Baedeker's

BARCELONA

Hints for using the Guide

Following the tradition established by Karl Baedeker in 1846, buildings and works of art, places of natural beauty, and sights of particular interest, as well as hotels and restaurants of especially high quality, are distinguished by one ★ or two ★★.

To make it easier to locate the various places listed in the "A to Z" section of the guide, their coordinates are shown in red at the head of each entry: e.g. Palau Nacional H–I 5.

Coloured strips on the right-hand side of the page are an aid to finding the main heading in the guide: blue stands for the Introduction (Nature, Culture, History), red for the "Sights from A to Z" section, and yellow indicates Practical Information.

Only a selection of hotels, restaurants and shops can be given; no reflection is implied therefore on establishments not included.

In a time of rapid change it is difficult to ensure that all the information given is entirely accurate and up-to-date, and the possibility of error can never be entirely eliminated.

Although the publishers can accept no responsibility for inaccuracies and omissions, they are constantly endeavouring to improve the quality of their guides and are therefore always grateful for criticisms, corrections and suggestions for improvement.

Preface

This pocket guide to Barcelona is one of the new generation of Baedeker guides.

These guides, in a convenient format, are illustrated throughout in colour, and are designed to meet the needs of the modern traveller. They are quick and easy to consult, with the principal places of interest described in alphabetical order.

Barcelona, the capital of Catalonia, rivals Madrid not only on cultural and economic grounds, but also because the extensive building work and infrastructure development carried out for the 1992 Olympic Games have given parts of the city a modern character.

Looking across the Exhibition Grounds to Tibidabo

The present guide is divided into three parts. The first part gives a

general account of the city – including population, government, language, economy, transport and culture. This is followed by an account of some famous people who were natives of Barcelona or who have been associated with the city, and a survey of its history.

A selection of quotations and suggested walks leads into the second part of the guide, in which the principal places of interest in Barcelona and its surroundings are described in alphabetical order. The third part, also arranged alphabetically, contains a variety of practical information, designed to help visitors to find their way about and make the most of their stay.

Baedeker guides concentrate on essential information and are user-friendly. This new guide is abundantly illustrated and contains a number of carefully revised plans and numerous colour photographs. At the back of the book is a comprehensive map and against each entry in the "Sights from A to Z" section are given the coordinates of the square of the map in which the particular feature can be located.

Contents

Baedeker Specials

Welcome to

Visitors to this seaward-facing capital of Catalonia are welcomed by a city that is not only bursting with pride and self-confidence, but also more than capable of competing with the Spanish capital Madrid located deeper inland. And since Spain experienced the drive for increased regional autonomy that gathered pace from the end of the 1970s, Barcelona has every justification for projecting itself as the fulcrum of a flourishing economic and cultural life.

Two periods in particular have coloured Barcelona's distinctive cityscape: the Gothic age, during which the medieval Old Town around the cathedral was developed; and the late nineteenth century, when unparalleled economic prosperity made possible, in a breathtakingly short space of time, the construction of a planned new town. Thus it was that, between the Gothic quarter and the flanks of the coastal hills, the grid pattern expansion of the city – the "Eixample" – emerged, on which "Modernisme", the Catalonian variant of Art Nouveau, left the profoundest imprint. Even today Barcelona delights in the fame of the unconventional architect, Antoni Gaudí, whose still incomplete masterpiece, the Church of the Holy Family, dominates the surrounding districts.

A joke
from the past –
the "Woman with
the Umbrella"
in the Zoo

The choice of Barcelona as the venue for the XXVth Olympiad was to prove a further equally powerful stimulus. The city aspired to present an expansive, handsome face, open and welcoming to the world; and by the time the Games

A modern landmark
for Barcelona is its
telecommunications tower

Light towers
in the Parc de l'Espanya
Industrial

Barcelona!

started this ambitious aim had largely been achieved. The years since then have seen the finishing touches applied to a number of large-scale projects initiated in this most recent of development phases.

Barcelona's museums include several which are truly world class, among them the Picasso Museum, the Miró Foundation, the Thyssen-Bornemisza Collection in Pedralbes, and the National Museum of Catalonian Art, with a collection of Romanesque murals which has few rivals.

Less highbrow forms of recreation are catered for by two areas of the city in particular. The first is Montjuïc, its slopes, falling steeply to the shores of the Mediterranean, being crowned with a fortress and covered with carefully tended gardens. Here the large amusement park and the Poble Espanyol (the "Spanish Village", laid out for the 1929 World Exhibition with reconstructions of historic buildings from all over the country), draw crowds of visitors from far and wide. Complementing Montjuïc is Tibidabo, part of the coastal hill chain, also with an amusement park and affording magnificent views of the city, sea and hinterland.

As if this were not enough there is also the Ramblas, the most famous of Barcelona's boulevards. Shaded with aged plane-trees and abuzz with open-air cafés, flower stalls and impromptu entertainment, it leads to the Old Harbour with its glittering new shopping and restaurant complex, the "Maremagnum", and Europe's largest aquarium, further enhancing the city's proud claim to be "Princess of the Mediterranean".

The coat of arms

of the Catalonian capital at the entrance to the Mercat de la Boqueria

Columbus Monument

pointing out beyond the sea

Flags in the wind

showing the Spanish and Catalonian colours

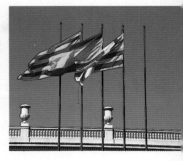

Nature, Culture History

Facts and Figures

Coat of arms of
Barcelona

General

Barcelona, the capital of the autonomous region of Catalonia
(Catalunya), lies 2°10'E (on the same meridian as Paris) and 41°23'N, in
the extreme north-east of the Iberian peninsula.
   Favourably situated on a broad coastal plain rising gently from the sea
up to Tibidabo, which is 532 m (1746 ft) high, the city is bordered on the
north-east by Muntanya Pelada and on the south-west by Montjuïc. On
the far side of Muntanya Pelada lies the gorge of the Riu Besos, while
south of Montjuïc the Riu Llobregat flows into a wide and fertile plain,
the market garden of Barcelona.

Not only is Barcelona the most important economic, communications,
educational and cultural centre in Catalonia, it is also now competing
successfully with Spain's capital city of Madrid in those fields. It boasts
several distinguished colleges and other educational establishments, an
archiepisopal see, a large number of museums, some of international
standing, important publishing houses, and is a stronghold of musical
and theatrical life. Recently, too, it has become a centre of industrial
design.

Cityscape

The face of the city has been moulded by three main phases in its history: the Roman period, extensive remains of which have been discovered beneath the medieval town centre; the mainly Gothic core of the
city; and finally the large scale development undertaken in the 19th c. As
Spain remained neutral in both world wars, and the Spanish Civil War
(1936–39), violent though it was, did not result in large areas of destruc-
tion, Barcelona has survived well architecturally.

The **Old Town** is bounded by the harbour, and by wide inner ring roads
("rondas") that have replaced the old walls. On the highest point in the
city centre, Mont Tabor (12 m (40 ft) high), stands the cathedral, surrounded by medieval alleyways. The main streets are the Ramblas, wide
tree-lined promenades that divide the Old Town into two parts, Barri
Gòtic and Barri Xino.

The newer districts, the **Eixample**, with their boulevards lined with plane
trees and their stately houses, have been built largely in accordance with

◀ *Plaça Reial: a peaceful square in the Old Town*

Barcelona	Location	2°10′E
Capital of the Spanish		41°23′N
autonomous region		
of Catalonia	Population	1.7 million

plans drawn up around 1860, with the roads laid out to a formal grid pattern. At that time too a number of small townships inland were incorporated into the city. Here will be found a surprisingly large number of important buildings falling into the Modernisme category (see p. 30), the Catalan equivalent of Art Nouveau. Avinguda de la Meridiana, coming from the north, exactly follows the line of the Greenwich meridian, while Avinguda del Paral·lel obtains its name from the fact that it runs parallel to the lines of latitude. The other main streets lie at angles of 45° to these; however, all street plans currently available show them as being exactly vertical or horizontal, which is not in accord with most other maps and can lead to confusion.

Society

The population of the city in 1989 was 1,707,286 (3.5 million including the suburbs). This makes Barcelona Spain's largest city after Madrid.

Population

The total is made up mainly of Catalans, together with some 760,000 Spaniards who have migrated from other – mainly more undeveloped – provinces, and about 42,000 foreigners from various countries.

In 1900 Barcelona had 537,000 inhabitants; by 1930 the million mark was passed and in 1979 the figure reached 1.9 million. Since then the population has remained relatively constant, with a tendency to reduce slightly. Some 23 per cent fall into the fifteen to thirty age group.

The Olympics and After

Both during the event and subsequently, the XXVth Olympic Games changed the face of Barcelona to a degree unparalleled in former times.

With the decision to hold the 1992 Olympics in Barcelona, a hectic and still continuing building programme unfolded. Intended to help the city's infra-structure to cope with the heavy demands about to be placed upon it, this inevitably meant permanent changes in the city's appearance. Under the slogan "Barcelona posa't Guapa" (Barcelona, make yourself beautiful), "Nou Urbanisme" took over everywhere in an effort to solve the problems arising from the inadequacy of existing structures. It goes without saying that compromises were needed if the city were not to forfeit its distinctive atmosphere and charisma.

Barcelona committed investment and ambitious ideas to expanding com-munications and the tourist infrastructure. In the process some two dozen high-class hotels were built; the airport at El Prat de Llobregat was extended; and the Estació de França (the main railway terminal for services to neighbouring France and farther north) was completely modernised; the Catalonian National Theatre and Auditorium are even now taking shape on the site of a former railway station on the Plaça de les Glóries Catalanes.

The port area too has profited from modernisation; the Moll de la Fusta, a promenade with restaurants, underground car park and subway, opened in advance of the 1992 Olympics. The old harbour basin of Port Vell has been transformed by completion of a shopping, cultural and leisure complex incorporating a huge cinema, modern aquarium and World Trade Centre, as well as a water-sports centre and all necessary facilities. Complementing this reconstruction of the old are new developments such as the Olympic Village, farther to the north-east, together with the Olympic Harbour (Nova Icaria) and Convention Hall.

In Montjuïc not only has the Palau Nacional been completely modernised but the Botanic Gardens have been newly laid out as well. Tibidabo is today graced by the Torre de Collserola, a 288-m (945-ft) radio tower providing an unrivalled panorama of the Catalonian capital.

The positive effects of the Olympic boom continue to be felt, proving them-selves more than just short term. The official accounts show that the full cost of redevelopment – estimated at approximately £5 billion – has been met without incurring substantial debts; indeed a surplus was recorded. In this the policy of enlarging and modernising existing stadia wherever poss-ible, rather than building new, was a major contributary factor. Last but by no means least, construction of capacious ring roads has succeeded in diverting a large proportion of through traffic away from the city centre.

It is clear that the city's numerous initiatives have paid off handsomely, most notably in enhancing Barcelona's attraction as an economic centre and so reviving the great economic tradition that, in earlier centuries, especially before the dramatic impact of the opening up of the New World, made Barcelona one of the major cities of the Mediterranean region.

Moll de la Fusta promenade

There has been a clear trend towards leaving the city. During 1989 less than 5500 people moved into Barcelona from the surrounding province, while 16,000 turned their backs on the city and moved out into the country.

By far the majority of the population are Roman Catholics, the remainder being made up of Protestant, Muslim and Jewish minorities.

Religion

Administrative districts

The city area of Barcelona, covering some 99 sq. km (38 sq. mi.), is divided up into ten districts, listed below in clockwise order, starting from the Old Town centre.

City

No.	Name	Population
1	Ciutat Vella	101,677
2	Eixample	287,948
3	Sants/Montjuïc	184,772
4	Les Corts	91,004
5	Sarrià/Sant Gervasi	154,523
6	Gràcia	133,146
7	Horta/Guinardó	191,532
8	Nou Barris	196,046
9	Sant Andreu	147,664
10	Sant Marti	218,974
Barcelona total		1,707,286

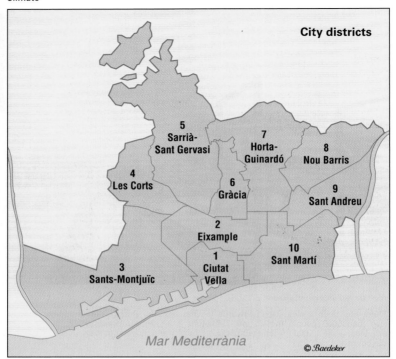

City districts

5 Sarrià-Sant Gervasi
7 Horta-Guinardó
8 Nou Barris
4 Les Corts
6 Gràcia
9 Sant Andreu
2 Eixample
1 Ciutat Vella
10 Sant Martí
3 Sants-Montjuïc

Mar Mediterrània

© Baedeker

Climate

Barcelona enjoys a fairly even Mediterranean climate, without excessive differences between minimum and maximum temperatures. The air temperature seldom falls below freezing point and hardly ever exceeds 35°C (95°F); during the day temperatures may fluctuate by between 6 and 15°C (11 and 27°F). The wind comes mainly from the south, and humidity is about 70 per cent in the lower parts of the city, reducing as the land gets higher towards the coastal mountains. When there is little wind the atmosphere in the inner city can become heavily polluted by exhaust fumes and industrial gases.

Culture

Education

The city is an important educational centre. Pride of place must go to the **University**, which offers courses in biology, law, economic sciences, pharmacy, philology, philosophy, physics, geography and history, geology, mathematics, medicine, education, psychology and chemistry. The university buildings are widely scattered throughout the city and its immediate suburbs, with the greatest concentration being in the Zona

Month	Mean temperature	Rainfall	Days of rain
January	10°C (50°F)	5·6 mm (0.2 in.)	3
February	11°C (52°F)	16·0 mm (0.6 in.)	6
March	13°C (56°F)	31·2 mm (1.2 in.)	8
April	13°C (56°F)	75·5 mm (3.0 in.)	13
May	18°C (65°F)	19·9 mm (0.8 in.)	4
June	21°C (70°F)	22·8 mm (0.9 in.)	7
July	25°C (78°F)	2·9 mm (0.1 in.)	5
August	25°C (78°F)	70·8 mm (2.8 in.)	8
September	21°C (70°F)	53·3 mm (2.1 in.)	9
October	18°C (65°F)	19·7 mm (0.8 in.)	4
November	14°C (57°F)	113·7 mm (4.5 in.)	13
December	12°C (54°F)	25·3 mm (1.0 in.)	8
Total		456.7 mm (18.0 in.)	88

Universitaria on the western edge of the city. At present some 60,000 students are registered. There are branches of the University at Lleida (Lérida) and Tarragona.

The second important educational establishment is the Unniversidat Autònoma de Barcelona (Bellaterra; about 24,000 students), situated to the north-west of the city in Sabadell and Cerdanyola. It specialises in economics and business management, information studies, politics and sociology, jurisprudence, philosophy, philology, and medicine.

Most of the buildings of the Universitat Politècnica de Catalunya are also to be found mainly outside Barcelona, in Sabadell, Terrassa, Manresa, Vilanova i Geltru and Lleida. It specialises in architecture, agricultural science, civil engineering and road construction, telecommunications, information studies, nautical science, cybernetics, educational science, motor engineering, textile and energy technology, among others. At present it has about 15,000 students.

Law and economics are taught at the Universitat Pompeu Fabra, a private college.

Other **colleges** include the Catalonian Medical Academy, the Law Academy, the Academy of Fine Arts, and the Pharmaceutical Academy.

In addition there are a number of training colleges, institutes offering correspondence courses, and adult education centres.

Barcelona has two **music colleges**, the Municipal Conservatoire and the Liceu Conservatoire, an opera house. In addition there are schools teaching theatre, dance and choreography.

The city boasts some fifty **museums**, some of world renown, such as the Museu d'Art de Catalunya (closed temporarily), the Museu Picasso and the Fundació Joan Miró. There are also a number of specialist museums, some of which are accessible only to qualified personnel. At the present time some museums are closed temporarily for renovation or remodelling, or offer viewing by prior arrangement only. For further details see Sights from A to Z.

Libraries Pride of place goes to the University Library, with some 1,600,000 volumes if its specialist branches are included. Also of considerable importance, especially as far as books in the Catalan dialect are concerned, is the Bibliotheca de Catalunya. In addition there are numerous local and children's libraries and those catering for specialist subjects as well as historical and scientific archives.

A group of stone Sardana dancers in front of the amusement park on Montjuïc

Publishing

Barcelona also enjoys a long and distinguished tradition in the world of publishing, founded on a determination – even during the Franco era – that Catalan literature would not be allowed to die. The city is the home of at least two hundred publishing houses, including some of Spain's most important book publishers. About a dozen daily newpapers are printed.

The annual "Liber" book fair is one of the most important events of its kind.

Music

Barcelona's musical tradition finds particular expression in two world-famous performance halls. The Palau de la Musica Catalana, a building of considerable architectural merit in the Modernisme style, has its own chamber orchestra and also offers a wide spectrum of music ranging from classical to experimental, jazz, pop and rock.

The Liceu is the largest opera house in Spain, and in the whole of Europe only La Scala in Milan can better it. It maintains its own orchestra, and performances normally start in late autumn. At the beginning of February 1994 however the Liceu was almost completely destroyed by fire. It is to be reopened in the autumn 1999.

Mention should also be made of the fact that the soprano Montserrat Caballé and the tenor José Carreras, both world-famous singers, both hail from Barcelona. Composed by Mike Moran for the inauguration of the 1992 Olympic Games and sung bu Montserrat Caballé and Freddy Mercury, the "Hymn to Barcelona" is today widely familiar.

Theatre

In conjunction with the present frantic rebuilding taking place in Barcelona, the National Theatre is going up near the Plaça de les Glòries Catalanes. Until it is opened theatrical performances are concentrated in some twenty five smaller theatres with varied repertoires.

The bigger banks and financial institutes, especially the Caixa de Barcelona and the Caixa de Pensions, are contributing a percentage of their profits to a large number of different cultural activities. For example, they are helping to maintain historically important buildings and finance museums and musical events.

Sponsorship

A literary event with a long tradition is Barcelona's "Jocs Florals" (Flower Games), a poetry competition which has been held every year since 1859 with the aim of promoting Catalan literature.

Jocs Florals

Language and Literature

As in the rest of Spain, Castilian (Castellano), or "high Spanish" is officially recognised as the prime language to be used in civil service and business circles in Catalonia. However, in Barcelona there has been a growing move for some years now to make Catalan the only language to be used officially; since 1975 it has become far more widely accepted in official circles and in schools, and has largely superceded Castilian. However, all Catalans are bilingual, and there is no need to learn Catalan specially for a holiday in Barcelona; a basic knowledge of Castilian will suffice, even though more and more road signs and other informative text may be only in Catalan. However, anyone with a knowledge of French will soon master it, but making yourself understood verbally has its difficulties because of the rather strange accent the Catalans have.

Language

Catalan, an original Romance language, displays considerable differences from pure Castilian and its vocabulary betrays a strong Provençal influence. In various dialect forms it is spoken by a total of some seven million people, in the Valencia region and in the Balearics as well as in Catalonia, and also in the foothills of the Pyrenees in eastern France, Andorra and even around the town of Alghero in Sardinia.

Unlike Castilian, Catalan lacks dipthongisation of the Latin root vowels (e.g. Latin portus, Castilian puerto, Catalan port; Latin bonus, Castilian bueno, Catalan bo). Final vowels disappear (e.g. Castilian dulce, Catalan dulc; Castilian muerte, Catalan mort). As well as the high Spanish verb forms ending in -ar, -er and -ir, Catalan has another form ending in -re (e.g. prendre, meaning "to take"). Examples of the Provençal influence on its vocabulary are words such as those for "table" (Castilian mesa, Catalan taula), "corn" (Castilian trigo, Catalan blat) or "window" (Castilian ventana, Catalan finestra).

Pronunication As in Portuguese, the unstressed a and e are almost swallowed, the unstressed o is short. The Castilian j as well as the g before e and i (pronounced like the Scottish ch in "loch" before a, o and u) become like the English j ("jug") in Catalan. Double L, roughly like ly in "badly" in Castilian, becomes more of a y in Catalan; where it is intended that it should be pronounced like a double l is in English the two letters are separated by a full stop or, occasionally, a hyphen. The Spanish letter ñ (pronounced roughly like ni in "onion") becomes ny, and Catalan knows no y as such; it is always written i. Ch is always hard, like k; nowadays c is nearly always used instead. The letter x always sounds like sh. The Castilian sound ch (like "chip") is replaced by tx, or often -ig at the end of a word. Z and c before e and i are not lisped as in Castilian, but are frequently pronounced more like an s. Catalan knows a double S (e.g., massa), whereas Castilian does not.

The rules for stress correspond to those used in high Spanish, except that in the ending -ia there is no stress on the i (Castilian María, Catalan Maria). According to how the vowel is pronounced, emphasis may be by means of a grave (`) or acute (´) accent: an à always takes the grave, ú and í the acute; e and o take the grave when the vowel is open (e.g., cafè, arròs), and the acute when closed (consomé).

Catalan literature

The first known examples of Catalan literature date from the 12th c. Historical works and chronicles cover a wide field, and there are numerous translations of the ancient classics and academic works from Moorish culture. On the other hand, original literary works are few and far between.

The poetry and literary works of the court troubadours from Provence, which flourished in the 12th and 13th c., had a considerable influence on Catalan authors, and many Provençal words and phrases found their way into the language. A central figure in Catalan language and culture was **Ramón Llull** (or Raymond Lully). Born on the island of Mallorca, he lived c. 1235–1316 and was a man of great education. Under him Catalan flourished as a cultural language to an extent it has not yet been able to match since. Lullus's essays, novels and poems, which have had such an important bearing on Western thinking, were written in his native idiom as well as in Latin and Arabic. As a result his works could be understood by the rank and file who understood only Catalan, as well as by the educated elite. He followed the idiom so closely that a Catalan can read his works today without any difficulty. Lullus's work "Libre de Cavalleria", the theme of which was how to lead the life of chivalry, was taken up by **Joanot Martorell**, who brought the Catalan romance of chivalry to its peak in his "Tirant lo Blanch" c. 1455. Mention should also be made here of the Valencian **Arnau de Vilanova** (c. 1240–1311), an equally learned and religious man.

From the 15th c. onwards the Iberian peninsula drew ever closer to Castile and the Castilian language; high Spanish is still known today as "castellano". As a result Catalan suffered a fate similar to that of the Provençal dialect which had filtered down from northern France, and with which it had so much in common; although it retained its importance as a spoken language it became supplanted by Castilian in the written word and, above all, in the literary sphere. In 1714, under a decree published by King Philip V, it was even banned from official use. This meant in practice that no original Catalan literature could be disseminated, and it was not until the Romantic period, with the reawakening of past values and a realisation of its true importance, that Catalan was reborn. It was introduced into literary and intellectual circles, received support from sponsors and was the subject of detailed philological research. The linguist Maria Aguiló (1825–97) produced the first "Dictionary of Classical Catalan"; Tomás Forteza (1838–89) published a "Gramática Catalana", and Joan Alcover came up with the "Diccionari de la Llengua Catalana" prior to 1906.

The 19th c. literature concentrated on subjects from middle-class life. Particularly worthy of mention are **Jacint Verdaguer i Santaló** (1845–1902), a distinguished epic poet, still highly spoken of today, **Emili Vilanova** (1840–1905), humorist and comedy writer, and **Pere Corominas** (1870–1939), who wrote under the pen-name of Enrique Mercador, well known as a political and philosophical writer and as a freedom fighter in the Spanish Civil War.

When Spain was being regionalised and suffered from separatist uprisings during the late 1970s Catalan – which has been recognised once more as an official language since 1975 – enjoyed a further boost. Today there are Catalan books, periodicals and newspapers; the Third TV programme often broadcasts in the Catalan language; road signs and place names have been changed; every bookshop has Catalan/Castilian dictionaries on sale – the list is endless. Recently scientific and academic books from abroad have been translated straight into Catalan, without first being put into Castilian. As a result of Catalan having been banned for so long in scientific circles it had inevitably failed to keep up with recent developments, so a whole new vocabulary covering modern terms had to be drawn up – in the same way that the Vatican was obliged to introduce new Latin words for such terms as "data processing", "atomic power" and "population explosion". There is one sphere that has remained unaffected by Franco's centralised cultural policy, that of local and regional history, where many historiographical works have been published solely in Catalan ever since the Renaixença.

However, as mentioned above, there is no need to worry about acquiring a knowledge of Catalan for your holiday. All mainland Catalans are bilingual, and most people working in tourist information offices, travel agents, hotels and restaurants and the larger shops speak English and/or French.

Customs

As in most other large European towns and cities, old customs and traditions have tended to die away to a large degree, so we will dwell only on a few key traditions that have survived and still play an important role in the lives of the people.

The Sardana is a typically Catalan round dance in three-quarter or five-eighth time, with a mixture of short and long steps and quick and slow time, and is today often to be seen danced on the streets and squares of Barcelona, for instance, in front of the cathedral or in Poble Espanyol. The music is based on popular tunes from the 16th and 17th c; instruments commonly used include flutes, oboes, trumpets, trombones, drums and double bass.

Sardana

A folklore speciality in the towns are the "giants" ("Gegants") – huge puppets in lavish costumes – who, on festival days, and specifically on Midsummer's Day, are carried through the carnival processions. On such occasions one can marvel at the "Castellers", and the groups of festively dressed men building high towers of people with acrobatic perfection.

Gegants and Castellers

Even though more and more criticism has been levelled in Spain of late at the bloody spectacle of the bullfight ("corrida de toros"), a visit to the arena is still one of the Spaniard's favourite leisure pursuits. Several pages in the newspapers are devoted to details of the fights and the toreros and the form of the animals. The visitor to Barcelona must make up his own mind whether he wishes to see a bullfight – he is bound to encounter one in some way or another.

Bullfights

Until the 16th c. bullfights were arranged in noble circles both as trials of strength and also at parties, the idea being that the caballero on horseback had to kill the bull with his lance. From the 17th c. onwards the fighting was done increasingly on foot; the rules used today are based largely on those drawn up by Francisco Romero, who was born about 1700 in Ronda.

In the round bullfighting arena the more expensive seats are on the shaded side ("sombra") and the cheaper ones on the sunny side ("sol"). The black and reddish brown beasts, which may not be more than six years old and weigh about 500 kg, come mainly from Andalusian breeders.

The fight ("lidia") is made up of three main parts ("suertes"). After a short preliminary skirmish, in which the capeadores tease the bull with their brightly coloured capes ("capa"), the mounted picadores commence the suerte de picar or suerte de varas, when they encourage the bull to attack them, pierce the enraged animal in the neck with their lances ("garrocha") and try to dull the force of its attack. When the bull is worn down ("castigado") by being speared by the lances ("varas") the second part of the show begins, the suerte de banderillas. The banderilleros approach the bull with several banderillas in

their hands and, swerving away at the moment he attacks, pierce him in the neck. The banderillas normally used are sticks 75 cm (30 in.) long, with barbs and decorated with spangles; banderillas à cuerta are only 15 cm (6 in.) long. If the animals turn out to be too quiet or too insidious the men try to annoy them by making passes with their capes ("floreos"). When the beast has three pairs of banderillas in its neck the suerte suprema or suerte de matar begins. The espada or matador, equipped with scarlet cape ("muleta") and rapier ("estoque") begins by teasing the animal with the cape. Finally he tries to get it into a suitable position to deliver the final thrust ("estocada"). A punterillo administers the coup de grâce with a dagger in the neck of the beast which, if it had put up a brave and aggressive fight, would then be loudly clapped and cheered. Clumsy bullfighters are booed and whistled.

The bloody spectacle may be repeated six or eight times until darkness falls.

Economy

Barcelona is the main **industrial centre** in Catalonia and, together with Madrid, the most important in all Spain.

At the top of the list stands the metal industry, followed by textiles, machinery and automobile manufacture, structural and civil engineering and road construction, paper manufacture and printing. In 1998 there were some 12,500 industrial firms in existence, predominantly small and medium-size undertakings.

Commerce far outweighs industry in Barcelona. In all there are some 37,000 firms operating in the spheres of wholesale (mainly textiles and leather goods, foodstuffs, technical equipment and road vehicles, furniture and household appliances) and retail trading (especially foodstuffs, textiles, shoes, chemical and pharmaceutical products, furniture, office supplies and printed items).

The **service sector** has developed into one of enormous significance. There are some 25,000 firms involved, of which more than a third are engaged in the hotel and restaurant trade, followed by transport, repair and servicing firms. Financial institutions and insurance companies also play a major role.

Transport

The whole of the city is very well served by **public transport**. Most local travel is by underground on the Metro, with five lines covering almost all of Barcelona. This is supplemented by local lines of the Ferrocarrils de la Generalitat de Catalunya (FGC), which serves the north-western outskirts and outlying areas, and also by trains belonging to RENFE, the Spanish state railway company, which run to the airport at El Prat de Llobregat, for example.

A complex network of bus routes and plenty of relatively cheap taxis mean that you can leave your own car behind if you wish when sightseeing in the city. In fact, such a course is to be recommended, because parking is very difficult indeed in the centre and unattended foreign vehicles are a target for thieves.

For more detailed information on transport facilities in Barcelona see Practical Information, Public Transport.

◀ *The famous "Castellers"*

Port Franc de Barcelona

Road network

The **streets** in the Old Town are mainly narrow and – like the wider boulevards in Eixample – many of them are one-way, making life difficult for anyone not familiar with the area. Road signs in the city are good and reliable.

Barcelona Airport is Spain's second largest after Madrid. It is about 10 km (6 mi.) south-west from the city centre, in the El Prat de Llobregat district. Some 8.5 million passengers are carried annually and 61,000 metric tons of freight. The building of a new terminal by early 1992 is expected to increase the number of passengers to 12 million per year.

For details see Practical Information, Air Travel.

The **port** (Port Franc de Barcelona) together with the outer harbour covers an area of about 300 hectares (750 acres). Once one of the major Mediterranean ports, it is still one of the most important in Spain.

In 1996 a total of 6555 ships put in here, a half of them from foreign parts. The total tonnage was 44.8 million gross metric tons. During the same period, the export tonnage was 6.5 million metric tons and the import figure 10.8 million metric tons; 361,000 passengers came to Barcelona by sea, and passenger and ferry services, mainly for tourists, also made an important contribution to the income of the Balearic Islands.

Famous People

The following is an alphabetical list of important people who were born, lived, worked or died in Barcelona and made a reputation for themselves elsewhere in the world.

The Catalan family names are shown initially in full, but subsequently abbreviated to their more common form in the text (e.g., Ildefons Cerdà i Sunyer becomes Ildefons Cerdà).

Nobody had a greater influence on the way Barcelona looks today than Ildefons Cerdà i Sunyer. After studying mathematics and architecture in Barcelona he went to Madrid in his twenties where he qualified as a roadworks engineer in 1841. His work as a civil servant took him to Tarragona and Girona and thence back to Barcelona, where he became deeply involved with town planning problems. In 1867 he published his "Teoria general de la urbanización" (General Theory of Town Planning), on the lines put forward by social Utopians. After fierce debate his plan for extending the city of Barcelona – taking due account of the social and infrastructural problems caused by the Industrial Revolution – was finally accepted in 1859 (see Sights from A to Z, Eixample).

His political career was just as important. As a member of the Progressive Party he was elected to the Cortes (the People's Parliament) in 1850 and in 1854 was made the city's legal adviser. The revolution of 1868, with the proclamation of a republic and the autonomous state of Catalonia, again put him in the political spotlight.

Ildefons Cerdà died in 1876 in Caldas de Besaya near Santander; in 1971 his mortal remains were taken to Barcelona and interred in the Cementiri Nou.

Ildefons Cerdà i Sunyer (1815–76)

Josep Clarà i Ayats was born in Olot, in the Pyrenean foothills of Catalonia, and received most of his artistic education at the academy of art in Toulouse in France. In Paris, where he moved to in 1900, he met the French sculptors Aristide Maillol, Antione Bourdelle and Auguste Rodin, all of whom influenced his future work. Also of significance was his friendship with the American dancer Isadora Duncan; his most original and dynamic drawings date from this period.

Josep Clarà received recognition as an artist at a comparatively young age; his design for the memorial to the Catalonian Volunteers in the Parc de la Ciutadella in Barcelona won him the Grand Prize in Paris in 1925; in the same year he was made a member of the Academia de San Fernando, the Royal Academy of Art in Madrid. At the 1929 World Exhibition he received the only Medal of Honour awarded on that occasion. After a short stay in Greece he finally moved from Paris to Barcelona. On the suggestion of his sister Carmen his house in Barcelona was made into a museum in 1969, and a considerable number of his works are still on exhibition there.

Josep Clarà i Ayats (1878–1958)

Born in Barcelona, Josep Comas i Solà soon made his mark as an astronomer; he was only fifteen when he published an article in a French specialist magazine. After studying mathematics and physics he obtained a position in 1904 at the Fabra observatory, where he remained as head of its astronomical department until his death. In 1911 he also founded the Spanish-American Astronomical Society and published hundreds of articles on popular science in the Barcelona press. He discovered two comets, one of which was named after him, and eleven planetoids, of which the one numbered 945 and conspicuous because of the strong path it follows is called Barcelona.

Josep Comas i Solà (1868–1937)

Famous People

Lluís Companys i Jover (1883–1940)

The politician and journalist Lluís Companys i Jover studied law at Barcelona University. He soon busied himself with political matters, founded the Associació Escolar Republicana in 1900 and worked closely with the youth organisation known as Unió Federal Nacionalista Republicana. He became editor in chief of the autonomist newspaper "La Barricada", worked on "Publicidad" and was also a founder-member of the Republican Party of Catalonia in 1917, whose tract "La Lucha" he published. He became a fervent supporter of the workers' demands, which led to his being arrested together with some friends of similar persuasion in 1920 and imprisoned in Mahón castle on Minorca. During the military régime under General Primo de Rivera he again became active as a lawyer and joined the Catalan opposition parties. He was arrested again in October 1930, only to be elected leader of the Barcelona city council in April of the following year. It was while holding that post that shortly afterwards he proclaimed the Catalonian Republic. Following the death of Francesc Macià in 1933 he took office as president of the Generalitat. When General Franco's troops entered Barcelona in 1939 he sought exile in France, was taken prisoner there by German troops and brought back to Spain. His strong involvement with the Catalonian Left led to his being court-martialled, and on October 15th 1940 he was shot in the fortress on Montjuïc.

Miquel Costa i Llobera (1854–1922)

The theologian and writer Miquel Costa i Llobera came from an aristocratic Majorcan family. During his student days in Barcelona he came into contact with Jacint Verdaguer, among others. His first works were published in 1873 in "Revista Balear", and the poem "El pi de Formentor" – still recognised as a masterpiece of Catalan poetry – caused quite a sensation in 1875. Technically speaking, most of his work was on ancient Classical lines; his influence on the Catalan language and its poetry is still felt today.

Lluís Domènach i Montaner (1850–1923)

Born in Barcelona, Lluís Domènach i Montaner was one of the architects who helped Modernisme in Barcelona to unfold in the unique way it did. After studying architecture in Barcelona and Madrid he received a professorship at the College of Architecture in his native city. The approach of the 1888 World Exhibition led to a flurry of building activity, and he seized the opportunity to submit his first important designs. Three times he received the prize awarded by the city of Barcelona for the finest building of the year, and three times he was elected president of the Ateneu, Barcelona's most important cultural body at the time. The thread running through his published writings was his strong allegiance to the cause of Catalan nationalism.

The most outstanding Barcelona building which he designed is the Palau de la Música Catalana, closely followed by the Hospital de la Santa Creu i de Sant Pau.

Antoni Gaudí i Cornet (1852–1926)

Antoni Gaudí, born in Reus in the province of Tarragona, is by far the most important Spanish architect of recent times. He was trained at the College of Architecture in Barcelona, at a time when Historicism and the Neo-Gothic were the very quintessence of all building. Gaudí was strongly drawn to Gothic, even though he strongly criticised some of its technical details, such as the use of buttresses, which he regarded as little more than crutches and wished to see replaced by sloping supports. His ideal was the reintroduction of a light, colourful Mediterranean form of Gothic, and such Gothic elements do in fact dominate many of his buildings. However, his very own creative design embraced the combining of historical patterns with plant forms woven in the Art Nouveau style, leading to the style known as Modernisme (see p. 30), which also made itself felt in the literary sphere.

Gaudí's principal works are found in Barcelona, where he built private residences, such as Casa Milà, Casa Batilò, and churches which on the one hand reflect Gothic forms, and on the other display a striking similarity to the designs of a Rudolf Steiner.

Gaudí received generous support and encouragement from the aristocratic industrialist Eusebi Güell, who asked him to design him a residence, the Palau Güell near the Ramblas, a country seat, Finca Güell and a housing estate for his workers, the Colonia Güell in Santa Coloma del Cervelló to the south-west. Gaudí's best-known building, however, is the Temple de la Sagrada Família in the north of the city; he devoted most of his working life to it, but this "Church of the Poor", as he called it, remains unfinished to this day.

Antoni Gaudí died as the result of a tram accident. Unrecognised, he was first taken to a hospital for the poor, and his true identity was only discovered just before he died.

It is impossible to imagine that architecture would have developed the way it did during the Modernisme period without Eusebi Güell i Bacigalupi, the extremely successful industrialist who was the great friend and patron of the architect Antonio Gaudí. After having studied political science, law and natural science in France and Great Britain as well as Spain, he founded the first Portland cement factory in Catalonia, ran a railway company and a bank, and went in for viniculture. Active too in the political field, he became a member of parliament for the province, a city councillor and senator. In 1900 he chaired the Jocs Floral de Barcelona, the poetry competition which had been set up in 1859 and is held every year. His house on the Carrer Nou de la Rambla, now the Theatrical Museum, was a mecca for well-known writers, painters, musicians and other aesthetes of the period. In 1918 he was elevated to the peerage.

Eusebi Güell i
Bacigalupi
(1846–1918)

For years a number of Mediterranean towns laid claim to having been the birthplace of the discoverer of America, but recent researches have established beyond doubt that he was born in Genoa. However, the exact date of birth of Christopher Columbus (Cristofol Colom in Catalan) is not known, but it was between August 25th and October 31st 1451. He became involved with seafaring and marine trade at an early age and came to Lisbon in Portugal in 1476, where he looked into the possibilities of finding the sea route to India, the existence of which had been known since ancient times, but the king showed no interest. On his way to France he passed through Spain where, in the monastery of La Rábida, the confessor of the Spanish queen Isabella gave him a letter of introduction to her. She agreed a contract with him for the voyage of discovery, and bestowed on him the ranks of grand admiral and viceroy of the region he hoped to discover. In addition he was to receive one-tenth of the anticipated profit from the venture.

Christopher
Columbus
(1451–1506)

On August 3rd 1492 the tiny fleet, made up of the caravels "Santa Maria", "Pinta" and "Niña", set sail on a westerly course from the port of Palos de la Frontera on the Atlantic southern coast of Spain, hoping to find India. For three long weeks the sailors saw nothing but sky and sea, and hopes of finding land grew dimmer and dimmer. The crew became restless, but after Columbus had altered course to south-west an island came into view, which he, on first setting foot on it, named San Salvador, although more than likely it was in fact Watling Island in the Bermudas. On the same voyage Columbus also reached Cuba and Haiti, where he left behind a group of 39 volunteers. He then returned to Spain in order to bring news of his success in person to the king and queen. In all he made three more journeys westward, without any real plaudits or financial gain being put his way in Spain; people were disillusioned by the fact that – instead of the legendary rich land of India being discovered – he had found only what they regarded as a rough, uncultured land inhabited by savages and with no real economic prospects. The crews who sailed with him also took it into their heads to denounce him and make things very difficult for him, even to the extent that, on his third voyage to Hispaniola (Haiti), he was seized and brought back to Spain in chains. However, he successfully defended himself before the

Famous People

king and queen and was rehabilitated. Nevertheless he never really received the honour his success warranted; even the New World which he discovered was named not after him but after a less important rival, the Italian Amerigo Vespucci.

At the 1888 World Exhibition the Columbus Monument was erected in Barcelona harbour, with his statue on the top of it. However, it faces the sea rather than the opposite direction towards America.

Ferdinand de Lesseps (1805–94)

The Frenchman Ferdinand de Lesseps, who built the Suez Canal, was his country's consul in Barcelona from 1842–48. People have not forgotten the way he came to the assistance of the city during the 1842 bombardment in which General Joaquin Alvarez Espartero suppressed a people's revolt. The uprising had come about as a result of a planned trade agreement with England which would have seriously hindered the industrialisation of Catalonia which was just beginning to take shape.

Joan Maragall i Gorina (1860–1911)

Born the son of an industrialist, Joan Maragall i Gorina, although a qualified lawyer, is best remembered as a writer. In 1890 he joined the editorial staff of the "Diario de Barcelona"; a year later his first poems and translations were published. Being financially independent he was able to devote himself to his literary ambitions, and his work as a journalist helped pave the way to Modernisme.

As a translator Joan Maragall was instrumental in introducing the works of such people as Goethe and Nietzsche to Spain.

Frederic Marès i Deulovol (b. 1893)

Born in Portbou, on the Franco-Spanish border, the sculptor and art collector Frederic Marès i Deulovol established one of Barcelona's most interesting museums. His travels took him to Brussels, Paris, Florence and Rome, and from 1946–64 he was the director of the Academy of Art in Barcelona. He has been responsible for the construction of a number of memorials.

Joan Miró (1893–1983)

Born in Montroig near Barcelona the artist Joan Miró was first inspired by the French Realists and, above all, by Cubism which was then just coming into its own and which he encountered in Paris on his first visit there in 1919. A little later he was one of the signatories of the Surrealist Manifesto; in 1923 he turned away from traditional painting and from Cubism and developed his own characteristic style. Miró's compositions display powerful and bold lines together with strong colours, with no suggestion of the abstract, and arouse many objective associations in the mind. He also worked with etching and printing techniques as well as in ceramics and sculpture. Until 1940 he lived mainly in Paris, but then fled back to neutral Spain when the Germans invaded the French capital. When Paris was liberated by the Allies in 1944 Miró was able to return to France. After the end of the war he moved to the island of Mallorca, where he died on Christmas Day 1983.

The Fundació Joan Miró on Montjuïc displays a most comprehensive collection of this artist's works.

Josep Pla i Casadevall (b. 1897)

Josep Pla i Casadevall came from the Baix Empordà region, and after studying law turned to journalism, initially with provincial publications. As foreign correspondent on various daily newspapers he went to France, Italy, Germany and the Soviet Union during the years 1919–39. It was during this period, too, that he published his first literary efforts, in the form of short stories, reports on his travels, and biographies. During the Spanish Civil War he lived mainly abroad, but returned to Catalonia in 1939. Although until then he had written mainly in Castilian, from 1945 onwards he turned completely to his native Catalan tongue, leavening the dialect and idioms of the region with plenty of his own linguistic imagination and vividness of expression.

Josep Puig i Cadafalch from Matató was the third great architect of the Catalonian Modernisme movement. Like Antoni Gaudí, he gained much of his inspiration from Gothic architecture, enriching it with local characteristics and much decoration. He was responsible in particular for a number of purpose-built industrial buildings, mainly for the 1929 World Exhibition, as well as collaborating in building on the Plaça de Catalunya and Via Laietana and in the archaeological digs which uncovered the ancient site at Empúries. He lectured at the Sorbonne in Paris and at Harvard University in the United States, and for a time worked on the Catalan newspapers "La Renaixença" and "La Veu de Catalunya". From the turn of the century he also influenced the region's educational policy.

Josep Puig i Cadafalch (1867–1957)

Born in Cubellas near Barcelona, the son of a family of Spanish artistes, Charlie Rivel, the "splendid acrobat", entranced circus audiences all his life. He was one of the "silent" clowns, whose jokes are never coarse and who amuse their audiences while awakening in them a feeling of melancholy and sympathy as a result of the tragic adversities which cause the clown all sorts of unhappiness, the like of which is only too familiar to us all. Charlie Rivel, whose hallmarks were an almost square red nose and a long, narrow pullover which came down below his knees, had the gift of making himself understood by those watching him without ever saying a word. He was a virtuoso of the onomatopoeic sounds with which he accompanied his act.
   A bronze statue to this world-famous artiste stands in the leisure park on Montjuïc.

Charlie Rivel (José Andreo Rivel; 1896–1983)

The architect Josep Lluis Sert i López is one of the leading men in his profession in Catalonia. He was strongly influenced by working with Le Corbusier in Paris in 1929–30 and also by the Bauhaus school of architectural design. The founding, with his support, of the GATCPAC (Grup d'Arquitectes i Tècnics Catalans per al Progrés de l'Arquitectura Contemporània) in 1930 formed part of the same line of thought. In 1937 he designed the Spanish Pavilion for the Paris World Exhibition; since 1945 he has drawn up plans for a number of South American cities. In 1953 he succeeded Walter Gropius as head of the Faculty of Architectural Studies at Harvard University, and ran his own architect's office in Cambridge, Illinois, with considerable success. Since 1955 he has established strong contacts in Europe again; the Fondation Maeght in St-Paul-de-Vence, in southern France, and the Fundació Joan Miró on Montjuïc have been set up.

Josep Lluís Sert i López (b. 1902)

A native of Barcelona, Antoni Tàpies is one of the most important artists of the present day. His early works were strongly influenced by the Surrealists, especially Joan Miró, a personal friend. At the start of the fifties Tàpies went to Paris and mastered the newly arrived Tachismus style of painting (from the French word "tache", meaning spot or fleck, thus painting by flicking the colour on to the canvas), a variation from the more formal method, which led from Surrealism to total Abstraction.

Antoni Tàpies (b. 1923)

His subjects – he often works more with coloured plaster, ceramics and other materials more akin to sculpting than painting – portray a most unfamiliar language of symbols and signs. Tàpies has also made a name for himself as a draughtsman and illustrator.

Periodic special exhibitions by the Fundació Antoni Tàpies display a selection from his many works.

Like Miquel Costa i Llobera, a close friend, Jacint Verdaguer i Santaló was both poet and churchman. As chaplain of the "Companyia Transatlàntica" he crossed the Atlantic nine times in less than two years; his epic poem "L'Atlàntida" became known throughout the world. His most successful years were those spent serving in the household of the Marques de Comillas de Barcelona, the owner of the shipping line. In 1884 he went on a "Grand Tour", taking him to France, Germany and Russia, and in 1886 he visited the Holy Land.

Jacint Verdaguer i Santaló (1845–1902)

At the age of forty he took stock of himself and decided to change his life completely and renounce his duty of obedience to the church. Such a radical change found favour neither with the Count of Comillas nor with the church hierarchy, and he was prohibited from saying mass. What had happened led to much public murmuring and he was reinstated in 1898. Jacinct Verdaguer counts among the most popular of Catalan writers of epic poetry, perhaps his most important work being his description of the customs, myths and legends of his homeland.

◀ *View of Montjuïc from the Columbus Monument*

Wonderland of Glass and Stone

Barcelona is the very fountainhead of Modernisme, a typically Catalan style of art which dominated not only architecture and arts and crafts, but also literature, music and dance at the end of the 19th and early 20th c. To describe it simply as "Catalan Art Nouveau" would be to do it less than justice, though the two movements were, broadly speaking, contemporary.

The origins of Modernisme are to be found in the Renaixença, or Renaissance, the period when Catalonia began to rediscover its own history, language and culture. A simultaneous sudden growth of the city's urban area and population in what was an era of industrial and economic prosperity, created a well-to-do middle class and money for extensive building projects and ambitious civic planning, all factors that fostered a sense of pride spreading far beyond the city and its environs. Barcelonans craved a city capable of competing with the finest in Europe; in addition, the 1888 Barcelona World Exhibition meant that the eyes of the world were upon it. Thus Modernisme evolved as an upper-class cultural phenomenon developing in tandem with the burgeoning sense of national pride and self-awareness felt by the Catalan people as a whole.

Modernisme as an art form was based primarily on Impressionism, while at the same time incorporating a richly varied amalgam of Historicism and Art Nouveau. Elsewhere in Europe these were often consciously separated, but in Modernisme, especially in the work of the architect Antoni Gaudí, they are more often found combined – with varying degrees of emphasis – in a single subject. The Eixample, the expansion of the city funded largely by the upper classes in the 19th c., and the vigorous programme of building for the 1888 World Exhibition, led to an unprecedented boom in Modernisme architecture, the results of which still dominate Barcelona today. Typical of the style is its espousal of freedom of architectural form, increasingly ignoring straight lines and symmetry and indulging – some would say to excess – in decorative, playful and even comic detail. The manner of its development was determined largely by the fact that, unlike so many previous artistic movements which found expression mainly in buildings serving a wealthy, upper-class elite, Modernisme was the experience of all classes in the course of their daily lives – in religious and secular buildings open to the public at large, and in purpose-built and functional architecture, even in such comparatively humdrum structures as offices and shops. The boundaries between architecture and fine art became fluid; many an edifice in the Modernisme style has more the appearance of a gigantic sculpture than a building.

The strangeness of Modernisme in the eyes of those from other parts of Europe or indeed elsewhere in the world, lies in the above-mentioned mix of different styles, together with an obvious tendency to over-elaboration and clutter. Not infrequently Gothic, Moorish and Baroque features coexist with soaring and extravagant Art Nouveau botanical shapes and designs – even on buildings of really quite modest dimensions.

No one has left a stronger imprint on contemporary Barcelona than Antoni Gaudí (1852–1926), the brilliant architect who was born in Reus in Tarragona province but who spent his entire working life in the Catalan capital and who has stamped his artistic style indelibly on the city's skyline. In addition to his masterpiece, the Temple de la Sagrada Família, the many buildings designed for his generous patron Eusebi Güell deserve special mention, including Casa Milà, Casa Batlló and Casa Vicens. Many of Barcelona's squares and boulevards are lit by candelabras designed by Gaudí, and the ornamental pavements in many parts of Eixample are also his work. What is most distinctive is the way he combined elements of Gothic style and construction (of which he was quite critical) with the soft lines of the contemporary art of the time flowering throughout Europe as Art Nouveau, Jugendstil or the Modern Style. He was also extremely talented mathematically, verifying his load calculations empirically with the aid of wire or string models.

Matching Gaudí in importance is Lluis Domènech i Montaner (1850–1920) who taught at the College of Architecture in Barcelona. He was responsible for an impressive number of functional buildings (mainly constructed for the 1888 World Exhibition) in addition to the magnificent Palau de la Música Catalana. The functional excellence of his Hospital de la Santa Creu i de Sant Pau, not far from the Temple de la Sagrada Família, set the standard for others. His designs won the prize for the most beautiful building in the city on no less than three occasions.

Somewhat less spectacular is the work of Josep Puig i Cadafalch (1867–1957). Although he mainly designed buildings for industrial and commercial use, he was also responsible for reshaping much of the Plaça de Catalunya and the Via Laietana which runs through the north-east of the city centre.

The blocks of houses on either side of the Passeig de Gràcia comprise the largest concentration of Modernisme buildings. Known as the Quadrat d'Or ("Golden Rectangle"), the area is protected by a preservation order.

The Casa Milà, disparagingly referred to as the "stone heap"

History

Prehistory

In the Riss-Wurm interglacial period *c.* 13,000 BC, people inhabit the region of present-day Catalonia, especially the area around the mouth of the Riu Ter. Until the 5th millennium BC the folk living here are hunter-gatherers, progressing in time to agriculture and livestock rearing and with it a more settled style of existence. In the 2nd millennium BC the bell-beaker culture evolves, spreading from the western Mediterranean to the rest of Europe.

There is early evidence indicating the presence of **Iberians** on the eastern coast of Spain. Some researchers believe them to be the predecessors of the Basques and probably related to the Berbers of North Africa. First traces of Iberian occupation are found near the later settlement of Barcino as well as other sites.

In the course of the 6th c. BC Celts cross the Pyrenees into Catalonia in several phases but are presumbly quickly assimilated. Subsequently a mixed Celto-Iberian culture develops.

Ancient history

6th c. BC

Some of the ports along the east coast of Spain, including Emporion (now Empúries or Ampurias) are colonised by Greeks from Magna Graecia, mainly Ionians from the Phocaean colony of Massalia (Marseilles). The Greeks however are soon driven further south by the Carthaginians who, following the First Punic War, extend their colonial influence northward to the Ebro; present-day Catalonia remains under the control of the Roman Empire.

A settlement, **Barcino**, is said to have been founded in 218 BC by the Carthaginian general Hamilkar Barkas (though he died in 229 BC).

In 201 BC the Second Punic War ends in victory for the Romans; under the peace treaty Carthage relinquishes its European conquests. A little later (197 BC) Rome establishes the provinces of Hispania Citerior, capital Tarraco (Tarragona), and Hispania Ulterior (today the Andalusia region). A series of risings by Iberian Celts (143–133 BC) impedes total subjection of the peninsula but not its swift cultural and linguistic Romanisation. In the 1st c. BC the Roman praetor Quintus Sertorius, a supporter of Gaius Marius, attempts to establish an independent Celto-Iberian state.

27 BC

Spain is divided into the provinces of Hispania Tarraconensis (in the north-east, centred on the present-day town of Tarragona), Hispania Lusitania (in the west, between the rivers Duero and Guadiana), and Hispania Baetica (the original Hispania Ulterior); then, under the emperor Augustus, the entire Iberian peninsula is incorporated fully into the Imperium Romanum. Barcelona becomes a Roman colony with the name of Colonia Julia Augusta Faventia Paterna Barcino.

Visigothic rule

AD 414

The Visigoths (West Goths) under King Athaulf advance into Catalonia ("Gotalonia") and make Barcino their capital. King Eurich, ruler of the

Visigothic kingdom of Tolosa, defeats the Suevi and establishes Visigothic rule throughout Spain (apart from the north-west). The conversion of the Arian Visigoths to orthodox Catholicism is followed by their speedy integration with the Romanised inhabitants.

Moorish rule

During the period of Arab rule, the Iberian peninsula flourishes economically and culturally. The Moors take the city of Barcino, renaming it Bardschaluna. Charlemagne establishes the Spanish March as a defensive outpost against the Moorish caliphate of Córdoba; Louis the Pious conquers Barcelona in 801 and makes it the capital of the March. Catalonia is linked with the south of France by the Strata Francisca.

716

In 874 Wilfred of Barcelona founds the independent county (earldom) of **Catalonia**. The first stirrings of Catalan nationalism are felt; the process of throwing off the French yoke begins.

Almansor ("the Victorious"), grand vizier of the caliph Hisham II, conquers Barcelona – the northernmost expansion of Moorish military power in Spain.
    Soon after the turn of the millennium the counts of Barcelona, Urgell and Besalú join forces with the bishops of Barcelona, Girona, Vic and Eine to wage a massive campaign against the caliphs of Córdoba.

Heyday of Catalonia

Under the joint rule of the brothers Berenguer Ramon I and Ramon Berenguer I, the territory of the county of Barcelona is enlarged. The marriage of Ramon Berenguer IV to an Aragonese princess unites Catalonia and Aragón. Alfonso I of Barcelona (Alfonso II of Aragón) extends Catalonia's dominion as far as the French regions of Béarn, Bigorre, Carcassonne, Béziers and Nîmes.

1018–76

Ruler of the Mediterranean

During the **Cathar Wars** (1209–29) the French lose many of their possessions in Catalonia. Barcelona begins to expand beyond its Roman walls.

Jaime I ("the Conqueror") seeks political expansion in the Mediterranean region. In 1229 he leads a successful punitive expedition against the Majorcan pirates and fights his way into Palma.

Pedro III ("the Great") annexes Sicily, which remains in the hands of the House of Barcelona until the 15th c. The vast royal shipyards (Reales Atarazanas) are built onto the port of Barcelona. The city develops into a flourishing commercial metropolis and one of the most important banking centres in the whole of Europe.

The Cortes (standing representatives of the Church, the secular nobility and the towns and cities) of Aragón, Catalonia and Valencia increasingly act in unison.

After 1307

The marriage of Ferdinand II of Aragón and Isabella of Castile unifies the formerly rival kingdoms. The rule of the **Catholic Monarchs** (Reyes Católicos) sees a transition to absolute monarchy, as a result of which the Catalan estates, stirred by a strong sense of Catalan identity, are driven to oppose the Crown (several uprisings, especially in the 15th and 17th c.).

The **Reconquista**, the restoration of Christian rule throughout Spain, is completed with the capture of Granada. Christopher Columbus, whose voyages of discovery and exploration prepare the way for the establishment of the Spanish colonial empire in America, receives support for his project from Isabella.

Charles I, a Habsburg, becomes king of Castile and Aragón. In 1519, following the death of his grandfather Maximilian I, he inherits the Habsburg territories; in Rome in 1530 he is crowned Holy Roman Emperor (Charles V).

1517

In the naval battle of Lepanto (Greek name Naupaktos) at the entrance to the Gulf of Corinth, the Turkish fleet is annihilated by Spanish warships aided by those of Venice and the Holy See. The Spanish fleet is commanded by Don Juan d'Austria, a half-brother of Philip II. This naval victory ensures Spain's dominance of the Mediterranean.

Catalonia in the Spanish Empire

17th c.

The substantially increased tax burden leads, from 1640, to unrest in Catalonia. Uprisings by the estates are not crushed until 1652. The Peace of the Pyrenees brings to an end Spain's war with France which has lasted since 1635. Under the treaty Spain cedes Roussillon and Cerdagne to France, causing the Catalan cultural sphere to be split either side of the Pyrenean chain.

Philip V withdraws all special privileges hitherto enjoyed by the Catalans. The Catalan language is proscribed in official circles and is replaced by Castellano, the official language derived from Castilian. In order to keep down the rebellious citizens of Barcelona a sizeable fortress is constructed at the port.

The abolition by Charles III of Castile's monopoly on overseas trade bodes well for the future economic development of Catalonia.

1834

The introduction of a moderately liberal constitution in Spain.

In the **First Carlist War** (1834–39), Don Carlo, Ferdinand VII's brother, being opposed to the regency of the Queen Mother, Maria Cristine of Naples, during the minority of Isabella II, declares himself king (Charles V). Despite the support of the Basque provinces as well as Aragón and Catalonia, the venture fails and in 1839 he is forced to flee to France.

In 1838/39 the first workers' guilds and consumer cooperatives are formed in Barcelona. The **Second Carlist War** (1847–49) and republican uprisings aggravate internal conflicts.

In 1859, after a lively debate, the plan for extending the built-up area of the city, drawn up by the building engineer Ildefons Cerdá, is accepted. As a result, in the following years, the **Eixample**, that extensive part of the city, with buildings largely in the Modernisme style, stretching from the Old Town to the foot of the coastal mountains, gradually takes shape.

The **September Revolution** of 1868 brings about the abdication of Queen Isabella II who goes into exile. Declaration of the first Spanish Republic.

The **Third Carlist War**, initiated by Don Carlos' grandson, is directed against King Amadeo I, son of Victor Emmanuel II of Italy, and against the First Republic proclaimed by the Cortes in 1873. Mass socialist risings in the city and surrounding areas.

1888

The **World Exhibition** in Barcelona brings extensive new building (with an emphasis on the new Modernisme style).

Original sketch by Ildefons Cerdá for the new district of Eixample

Towards Catalan autonomy

After 1890 **independence movements** proliferate in Catalonia, Galicia and the Basque country. In 1906 the first congress to promote the use of the Catalan language is held in Barcelona. One of its main aims is standardisation of Catalan which, since the 17th/18th c., has existed only as a spoken language (Philip V having revoked all special Catalan privileges in 1714).

The founding in 1907 of the Institut d'Estudis Catalans (Institute of Catalan Studies) reflects the growing importance of Catalan, which is gradually becoming accepted in official quarters.

Following Franco-Spanish agreement (1904) on the countries' spheres of influence in North Africa, Spanish campaigns in Morocco lead to violent protests. The **Barcelona General Strike** is put down with much bloodshed.

Founding of the Catalan Mancomunitat (self-government with the emphasis on cultural autonomy). Self-government is revoked again in 1925. Spain remains neutral in the First World War. — **1914**

With the approval of Alfonso XIII, General Primo de Rivera establishes a military dictatorship. Dissolution of the Cortes. — **1923**

In 1929 another World Exhibition is held in Barcelona.

Following the Republican victory in the 1931 local government elections, Alfonso XIII leaves the country. Inauguration of the **Second Republic**. The liberal-progressive constitution provides *inter alia* for autonomy for Catalonia and in 1932 this becomes law. The Catalan language is authorised for use in official organisations and schools, and an increasing number of newspapers and books appear in Catalan.

The **Spanish Civil War** breaks out in 1936 following the murder of a Monarchist member of parliament, Calvo Sotelo, and the military rebellion in Spanish Morocco led by General Francisco Franco y Bahamonde. Franco and other generals set up a rival government in Burgos.

Franco era

In 1939 Franco's troops occupy Catalonia. The Franco dictatorship revokes the autonomous powers granted to the Catalans in 1932.

During the Second World War Spain again remains neutral in spite of its links with the Berlin-Rome axis. In 1940 Lluis Companys, republican president of the Comunitat, is court-martialled by Franco's troops and shot in the fortress on Montjuïc.

A national referendum in 1947 approves Franco's plan to restore the monarchy at a later date.

In 1966 the monastery on Montserrat launches a monthly religious tract "Serra d'Or", the first publication in Catalan since 1939.

Regionalisation

On the death of Franco in 1975, Prince Juan Carlos becomes **King Juan Carlos I** of Spain. The Catalan, Basque and Galician languages are authorised for official and educational use. In 1978, after a plebiscite, a new democratic constitution comes into force; Spain becomes a consti-tutional monarchy.

In a referendum held in 1979 Catalans vote in favour of far-reaching pro-posals for regional self-government. In November, by majority decision, the Spanish Lower House passes a **Statute of Autonomy**. The following year a regional parliament is elected in Catalonia.

1986   On October 17th Barcelona is nominated host city for the XXVth Summer Olympics in 1992, bringing massive inward investment and initiating an immensely vigorous programme of expansion and redevelopment.

1987   On June 19th the militant Basque separatist organisation ETA plants a bomb in a Barcelona department store, killing fifteen people and injur-ing many more.

The arrival of the Olympic Flag from Seoul (South Korea) on October 9th 1988 heralds the official opening of the **Cultural Olympiad** in anticipation of 1992. Queen Elizabeth II visits the Olympic site on Montjuïc.

On July 25th 1992 the **XXVth Olympic Games** open in the Olympic sta-dium. The "Hymn to Barcelona" recorded by the Catalan soprano Montserrat Caballé and the pop star Freddy Mercury (who was to die soon after), proves a triumphant success.

1994   In January Barcelona's historic Liceu opera house is gutted by a fire which starts during welding. Thanks to the many spontaneous offers of help rebuilding is able to begin almost immediately.

1996   In July–August the Jubilee Congress is held to mark the centenary of the International Publishers' Union.

The gala reopening of the **Liceu** opera house, now generously restored following the fire of 1994, is planned for autumn 1999.

Barcelona in Quotations

The Ramblas, the streets which lead from the harbour to the city centre, are narrow, old and friendly. A tree-lined avenue runs down the middle with chairs scattered about where you can sit and dream, and immediately you know that this is an ancient city-state, a polis. Men stand around in conversation and sit arguing under the trees. Their gestures are expressive and yet have a certain dignity. This one could be Demosthenes, that one Kleon, the tanner. This is how political parties were once formed and tyrants toppled. But their conversation is not concerned with politics; waving a rolled-up cycling newspaper they are discussing the football results. The policemen, armed with machine guns, guarding the main entrance to the police station, sit enjoying the shade like the cat among the mice next to them ...

Wolfgang Koeppen German author (b. 1906)

At this hour of the day the houses are like cool fortresses protected against the sun. The darkened rooms are cosy and pleasant. Perhaps Pan with his magical shepherd's crook and the ancient wisdom of leisure has crossed the Mediterranean. But at five o'clock Mercury awakes. The streets come to life. The bells of the old tramcars ring. Cars rattle by. The newspaper vendors raise their loud voices. The siesta is over and like everywhere else they try to cheat the customer ...

Among the confusion of these narrow streets [Barri Gòtic] stands the Cathedral. It seems more Moorish than Gothic. The visitor is guided by colonnades to a palm courtyard. The palm trees are so close together that their crowns touch each other forming a shady roof like that of a dense primeval forest. There is a pond beneath and behind a decorative wrought-iron grille white geese stretch their necks like stupidly arrogant guardians. The nave is as gloomy as the bottom of the sea. The Cathedral is a former mosque. Its columns are like stone palm trees which intertwine to form the roof, casting its heavy shadow over the choir and altar, over the worshippers in communion and the priests in their vestments. Everything is enveloped by the dark shadows and each candle creates its own little glow in the mountain of darkness ...

What else is there to see? The church of the Sagrada Família by Antonio Gaudí, a Barcelona architect, who even after his death is considered to be more progressive than Le Corbusier. His cathedral is built in the style of an Expressionist sugar baker, a fairytale tower for worshippers and much more friendly than the other churches in the city. Gaudí must have been a jovial man. He has built a house in a main street in the form of waves with the inhabitants looking out of the windows like despairing swimmers.

"Barcelona at Different Times of Day" (1958)

Around midnight we went down to the folk festival in Güell Park. The word "park" sounds harmonious and peaceful. It conjures up images of quiet avenues with graceful women and babies dressed in white, even green trees. In Güell Park you can forget these ideas. I don't know whether the name Güell sounds more attractive in Spanish than it does to North European ears. Utrillo's idea to take us to the park at midnight when bourgeois people like us have usually been in bed for ages was in

Julius Meier-Graefe German author (1867–1935)

itself suspicious. And especially in Güell Park. The last syllable contradicted everything that was suggested by the first. I couldn't help imagining something bizarre. This was unfortunate for I believe that without being prepared at all, it could be a great shock in the middle of the night ...

Finally, it must have been two o'clock, we reached a sort of cave or rather a temple or a giant carousel which was stationary. It was supported by columns which ressembled elephant teeth or whalebones. From there a path bordered by steep slopes that were littered with skulls or whatever, led to a plateau that on closer inspection turned out to be a hanging garden and was the roof of the temple in which we had been earlier. Then we came to a flower bed, which was a kilometre wide and closely packed with people instead of flowers. Next to it was another flower bed, and so on. I don't know how many. The monstrous things seemed to hover in the air and the people in them were unaware of the danger. In any case we had not enough time to think about it, for in a flash we faced another incredibly shaped building, half Indian Palace, half dog-kennel, made from faience or glass or soap bubbles. Utrillo told us calmly about Catalonia, as if we were sitting together quite normally. I pulled myself together, remained still and eagerly took in the closest details of a spittoon or monument. It was real faience and in the shapes I easily recognised traits of Horta and Guimard [well known Art Nouveau architects]. The memory of a house [Casa Mià] which I had seen days before in the Gracia came to my aid. I was not in a trance but in modern architecture. Oh, how I regretted all I had thought against Horta and Guimard, Endell and Obrist and whatever else the miscreants are called. Besides the ideas of this monster they all seemed like peaceful classicists. Utrillo explained that this man was going to build a cathedral and had many commissions. Barcelona was divided into two parties, those against him, those for him. He was a man of great energy and he still had a long way to go.

"Spanish Journey" (1910)

Wolfgang Weber
German journalist

With an almost irrational sense of liberality, which in other countries would long since have been inhibited by calculation and deliberation, the unheard of is performed daily in Barcelona. And it is this very irrationality and daring which gives the town the mark of the unusual. Or is it not of unparalleled audacity for a strict Catholic country to recklessly build a road through the palaces and churches of the Old Town to the harbour? And it is far-sighted, almost beyond our comprehension, to be already building the underground below a new suburban road, where there are no houses, but where it will one day be needed.

How does Barcelona evolve? For example: when a new road is being built in the inner city they continue building it at its full width out into the unpopulated countryside. Right up to the point where the fields begin it is immaculately concreted and provided with tram lines and carefully nurtured plane trees. And on this road a house is built, a palace with ten storeys, a dozen shops on the ground floor and all modern conveniences. A house and a road – that should be sufficient impetus to carry on building, to tempt the inhabitants of the dirty city, and at the same time to contribute to the outskirts looking the same as the inner city. "In the beginning the road" – Californian law on European soil!

In the inner city – the same largesse. The new town is strictly divided up into square blocks, not by narrow streets as in America, but by 60-metre wide avenues of plane trees.

The gigantic Plaza Cataluña arose through the demolition of an entire residential quarter and was excavated to form the underground railway station. The fire-damaged harbour district of Barceloneta was not salvaged but torn down and rebuilt at the city's expense. Barcelona is one of the few cities of the world that has an underground system; tram cars with electric doors; twice as many cars as the entire Hamburg area; and is building two new concourses onto the old one of a railway station, although there are only nine trains a day. Everything is larger than life, everywhere one expects developments to exceed those which have gone before.

"Barcelona" (1928)

I ambled further and ended up in a street which was even narrower and more crowded than the one I had come from. I shall call it the street of churchgoers. Here, squeezed in between high houses is Barcelona's cathedral which is so unimpressive and lacking in greatness that you can pass by it without even noticing it. It is the same as with many famous personalities: someone actually has to touch you on the arm and point them out to you. The crowd jostled me on the arm and I was pushed through the small door into the open arcade, which adjoins the church with a row of altars and encloses a courtyard of orange trees, planted at a time when a mosque stood here. The waters of the great marble basin where the Moors used to wash their faces before and after prayers still splashed. In the centre of it stood a pretty small bronze statuette of a rider on horseback with water spurting up around it. Closeby goldfish swam among luxuriant water plants and behind the grille geese were swimming, I would rather have said swans but one must keep to the truth if one wants to be an original travel writer. Riders in fountains and live geese were not conducive to worship and yet although there was so much else here the atmosphere was dominated by the ecclesiastical. Before the altars of the arcade people knelt in worship and incense streamed from the large open doorway of the church with organ and choirs resounding. I entered. Underneath the mighty arches there was a sense of gravity and greatness, yet God's sunlight could not penetrate the painted windows. The brooding half-darkness made denser by the incense was too oppressive for my thoughts of God. I longed for the open courtyard, whose ceiling is the sky, where the sunbeams fall between orange trees and rippling water. It was outside where the pious knelt, that the full gentle sounds carried my thoughts upwards to God and I first experienced divine worship in Spain.

I left the church and came through the narrow street into another that was equally narrow, yet shining with gold and silver. In Barcelona and several other Spanish cities things have not changed since the Middle Ages with the various craft guilds, for example, the shoemakers and the metal workers each having their own street where they sell their wares so that the whole range is on display. I found myself in the street of the goldsmiths. Here, one shop after another was full of gold chains and beautiful jewellery.

"Impressions from Spain" (1866)

Hans Christian
Andersen
Danish writer
(1805–75)

Walks

1. Port area and Nova Icaria

This circular walk starts at the Columbus Monument on the Plaça Portal de la Pau. A few steps away, in the direction of the sea, the Port Authority's (Autoritat Portuaria) somewhat over-ornate building stands at the landward end of the Rambla del Mar, a broad new pontoon bridge across to the Moll d'Espanya. Situated here are the Maremagnum, the huge Centre de Mar Aquari (aquarium) and Barcelona's IMAX cinema – not to mention two yacht clubs, the Reial Club Maritim and Reial Club Nautic – making the Moll d'Espanya the major attraction in the Old Port.

From the northernmost corner of the commercial port cut diagonally across La Barceloneta with its beachside bars and fish restaurants, then proceed along the Passeig Maritim – or the wide sandy beach running below and parallel to it – to Nova Icaria and the new Port Olimpic, with its equally new shopping, leisure and hotel complex of extravagant design. There are numerous fish restaurants and a well-appointed marina for leisure craft.

Leaving the Port Olimpic cross the Cinturo Litoral and go past the Vila Olimpic making for the zoo entrance on the north side of the Parc de la Ciutadella (Carrer de Wellington). Also in the Parc are the Museu d'Art Modern and, in the west corner, the Museu de Geologia and Museu de Zoologia.

From the splendidly modernised Estaciò de França (the mainline station north) and/or the Mercat del Born, a former market used nowadays as a cultural centre, it is only a short walk back to the port area. On the way a detour can be made through the alleyways of the Old Town to the Museu Picasso and Museu Textil.

2. From the port to Montjuïc and the Plaça d'Espanya

This walk also starts from the Plaça Portal de la Pau. First proceed the short distance to the intermediate station of the harbour Transbordador Aeri (on the Moll de Barcelona) and take the cable car up to the Plaça de l'Armada halfway up Montjuïc (check operating times in advance).

Alternatively, having first visited the Museu Maritim, continue on foot along the Avinguda del Paral·lel to the funicular railway up Montjuïc (terminus near the Metro station Paral·lel).

Close by the Plaça de l'Armada is the upper entrance to the Jardins Costa i Llobera, noted for its varied collection of cacti and succulents. Leaving the Plaça de l'Armada follow the Avinguda de Miramar to the continuation of the Montjuïc funicular, enjoying along the way some delightful views over the city; the cable car climbs above the Parc d'Atraccions and then up to the fortress on the top of Montjuïc. The descent can be made either through the amusement park or through the Jardins Verdaguer and so back to the Avinguda de Miramar. Further on, all well worth visiting, are the Fundaciò Mirò, then on the left the extensive Olympic site, and on the right the Palau Nacional with its world-famous museum of Catalan art.

From the Palau Nacional there is a choice of two routes: the first leads to the Archaeological Museum and then via steps to the Exhibition Grounds (also reached direct from the Palau Nacional); the second skirts the Olympic site before doubling back towards the city via the Poble

Espanyol and Pavelló Mies van der Rohe. Both routes converge on the Avinguda de Reina Maria Cristina, the fountain-lined main avenue running through the Exhibition Grounds to the Plaça d'Espanya, from where the Metro (Line 3) can be taken back to the Portal de la Pau.

3. Through the Eixample

Start at the Plaça de Catalunya on the northern edge of the Old Town from where the wide and exceptionally fine Passeig de Gràcia extends north-westwards into the Eixample, the grid-pattern extension of the city, built in the 19th c. Continuing along the boulevard note in particular the Casa Batlló on the left (in the Mansana de la Discordia) and then, on the right, the Casa Milà (La Pedrera). Crossing the broad Avinguda de la Diagonal with its unceasing flow of traffic, walk to the end of the Passeig and into the somewhat narrower Carrer Gran de Gràcia. In a side street, hidden in the maze of alleyways of what was once the village, now suburb, of Gracia, is the Casa Vicens, a relatively early design by Antoni Gaudí.

Return next to the nearby Metro station Fontana, take the Metro (Line 3) to Diagonal and change onto Line 5 in the direction of Horta. Alight at the next stop but one for a visit to the most famous building in Barcelona, the Temple de la Sagrada Família (open to visitors).

From there continue on foot along the wide Avinguda de Gaudí to the Hospital de la Santa Creu i de Sant Pau, a masterpiece of Modernisme built around 1900. Afterwards return by Metro to the starting point of the tour in the Plaça de Catalunya (Line 5 from Hospital de Sant Pau, changing at Diagonal to Line 3 in the direction of Zona Universitaria).

4. Old Town

See Barri Gòtic

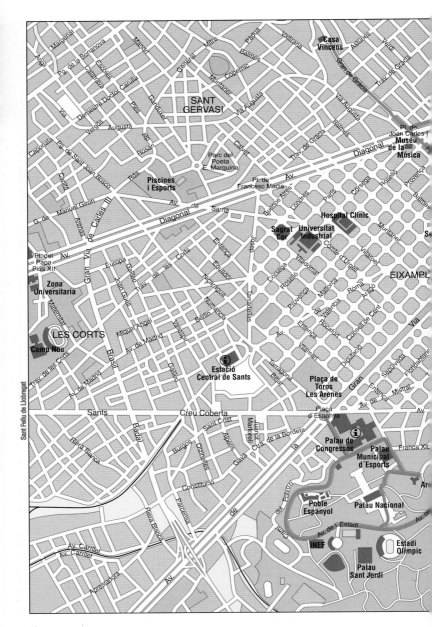

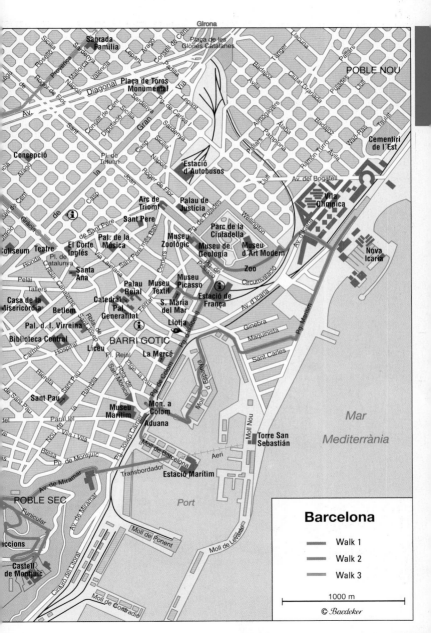

Sagrada Família

Plaça de les Glòries Catalanes

POBLE NOU

Plaça de Toros Monumental

Diagonal

Gran

Concepció

Estació d'Autobusos

Cementíri de l'Est

Av. del Bogatell

Arc de Triomf

Palau de Justícia

Sant Pere

Vila Olímpica

Museu Zoològic

Parc de la Ciutadella

Nova Icaria

Pal. de la Música

El Corte Inglés

Museu de Geologia

Museu d'Art Modern

Teatre

Coliseum

Zoo

Santa Ana

Circumval·lació

Museu Textil

Casa de la Misericòrdia

Palau Reial

Museu Picasso

Estació de França

Betlem

Caterdral

Pal Generalitat

S. Maria del Mar

Pal. d. l. Virreina

Llotja

Biblioteca Central

BARRI GOTIC

Liceu

La Mercé

Sant Pau

Museu Marítim

Mon. a Colom

Sant Carles

Maquinista

Ginebra

Aduana

Torre San Sebastián

Mar Mediterrània

Estació Marítim

Aeri

POBLE SEC

Transbordador

Port

Moll de Ponent

Moll de Levante

accions

Castell de Montjuïc

Moll de Contradie

Barcelona

— Walk 1
— Walk 2
— Walk 3

1000 m

© Baedeker

**Sights
from A to Z**

Sights from A to Z

Advice

Most commercial **plans of the city** of Barcelona and also the large plan contained in this guidebook are normally not orientated towards the north, but are printed in such a way that, for example, the streets in the extension of the city area known as Eixample run parallel to the grid of the plan. This can be somewhat confusing and may cause a visitor difficulty in getting his bearings.

The correct topographical situation can be seen on the small general plan on pp. 42–43.

The coordinates printed in capital letters against the main headings refer to the large city plan at the end of this guide.

The names of streets and Metro (underground) stations in Barcelona are signed exclusively in Catalan, as are almost all public buildings, monuments, etc. Consequently in the following chapter the names of such places also only appear in Catalan.

The names of Metro and railway stations dispense with specific expressions such as "Plaça" (square), "Carrer" (street), "Passeig" (promenade) or "Avinguda" (avenue); therefore when referring to these the same principle applies: for example the Avinguda del Paral·lel is referred to by the shortened form "Paral·lel". This actually matches standard postal practice.

Thanks to the frequency of its services and the compactness of its network, the Metro (underground) is the most comfortable method of **public transport** available. In addition, however, buses and trains (Ferrocarrils de la Generalitat de Catalunya) operate services in the city centre area, starting points for which are in the Plaça de Catalunya (Plaça d'Espanya for trains to Montserrat).

Arc de Triomf   H 11

Location
Passeig de Lluís
Companys

Metro
Arc de Triomf (L1)

The Arc de Triomf (**triumphal arch**) forms the main architectural feature of the spacious Passeig de Lluís Companys, which runs from the Parc de la Ciutadella (see entry) in a north-westerly direction. It was erected as the prestigious main gateway for the World Exhibition of 1888 by Josep Vilaseca. The brickwork incorporates elements of Moorish style; the reliefs depict allegories of trade, industry, agriculture and art. It has recently been restored at a cost of 120 million pesetas.

Architects' Society Building   I 10

Location
Plaça Nova

Opposite the main façade of the cathedral (see entry) and on the far side of the Plaça Nova stands the Col·legi d'Arquitectes (Society of Architects). The building, one of the first high-rise blocks in the city, was erected in 1962. On the side overlooking the square there is a triptych of graffiti friezes based on sketches by Pablo Picasso. The middle section depicts the "Gegants" (larger-than-life human figures who are

◀ *The entrance to the Parc Güell*

Arc de Triomf, main gateway to the World Exhibition of 1888

Graffiti, based on a Picasso drawing, on the Architects' Society Building

Badalona

Metro
Liceu (L3)

led out at popular festivals) and figures with palm branches; the left-hand section (on the Carrer dels Arcs) symbolises the joy of life, while the right-hand section (on the Carrer dels Capellans) shows the "frieze of standards". Inside the building are two more wall paintings by Picasso.

Badalona   outside the city plan

Location
NE of the city

Metro
Joan XXIII,
Sant Roc,
Gorg, Pep Ventura
(L4)

The industrial town of Badalona (pop. about 200,000) lies to the north-east of Barcelona and on the far side of the Riu Besos. Today Badalona has become practically part of the Catalan capital.

The city area extends some 5 km (3 mi.) along the flat coastline. The quality of the sea water suffers in this area as a result of emissions from the various industries. In the old town centre stands the **Church of Santa Maria**, dating from the 17th c. (works by the Baroque painter Antoni Viladomat). Roman remains are to be found in the town's Archaeological Museum (**Museu de Badalona**, Plaça Assemblea de Catalunya 1).

Sant Jeroni de la Murtra

About 3 km (2 mi.) to the north-west of Badalona lies Sant Jeroni de la Murtra, which with its former monastery, built in the 14th c. (15th c. cloister), is a favoured destination for outings from the town.

Montgat

About 3 km (2 mi.) to the north-east of the town, in Montgat, is a castle which played an important part in the War of Liberation fought against Napoleon (1788–1808).

Barceloneta   J–K 10–11

Location
NE of the port

Metro
Barceloneta (L4)

The district of Barceloneta (**Little Barcelona**) extends to the north-east of the harbour basin, which separates it from the sea. It was built from 1753 onwards and was laid out with a regular ground plan of intersecting streets crossing one another at right angles – a typical Baroque arrangement. Philip V's victory over the Catalans (1714) and the building of the Citadel (see Parc de la Ciutadella) had already taken place. Barceloneta was intended to provide new dwellings for those citizens who hitherto had lived on the site of the Citadel. Even today Barceloneta is above all others the area of the city with a pronounced maritime character; here is the Museu Marítim (see entry) and a number of good seafood restaurants.

Sant Miquel del Port

On the Plaça de la Barceloneta stands the Church of Sant Miquel del Port, which dates from the district's beginnings and which, in the arrangement of its floor space and façades, has strong affinities with the Italian Baroque style. To the right of the church façade is the house where Ferdinand de Lesseps lived in 1858 (memorial plaque).

The wide Passeig Marítim runs along Barceloneta's seashore. Stretching out to the north-east, the **beach**, with its broad expanses of fine sand, is a very popular place for relaxation and recreation. Care is taken to maintain the quality of the water at a high level, despite the beach's proximity to the city and its industrial installations.

Parc de Mar

The Parc de Mar, a spacious area of land in the north-east corner of Barceloneta, is where the Olympic Village, with its pair of distinctive high-rise towers, has been built. The yachting harbour is also located there (see Nova Icaria).

The **Passeig Joan de Borbó Comte de Barcelona** (formerly Passeig Nacional), which separates Barceloneta from the rest of the port area, leads from the Moll de Barceloneta southwards to the Torre de San Sebastián, a 96-m (315-ft) steel pylon which is the terminus for the harbour cable car (see Port) from Montjuïc (see entry).

★Barri Gòtic   H–I 9–10

The Barri Gòtic (**Gothic Quarter**) extends from the port to the cathedral and from the Ramblas as far as the Via Laietana. It is the oldest part of the city and acquired its distinctive character chiefly during the Gothic period when Barcelona, Genoa and Venice were the most important and prosperous merchant cities in the Mediterranean. However the roots of the city can be traced back to Roman times. Parts of the city wall date from this period and numerous remains of it can be seen.

Location
NE of the
Ramblas

Plan p. 50

For two thousand years the Barri Gòtic has been the spiritual and secular heart of the city. On Mont Tabor, at 12 m (40 ft) the highest point in the old city, stands the cathedral, surrounded by medieval alleyways. Close by lived the counts of Barcelona and the kings of Catalonia and Aragón. Christopher Columbus was received here by the Catholic Monarchs after his first voyage of discovery, and since the 14th and 15th c. the city and provincial administrations have had their seat here. Today the Barri Gòtic is mainly pedestrianised, with shops selling fashion goods, jewellery, antiques, books, souvenirs and ceramics; there are also a number of small bars and restaurants.

Tour

The starting point of the suggested tour of the Barri Gòtic is the Plaça de Sant Jaume, where stand the Casa de la Ciutat and the Palau de la Generalitat (see entries). On the north side of the square, the first building on the left in Carrer Jaume I houses the Museu d'Holografià (see entry). A short distance east, on the far side of the Plaça de Sant Just, is the Galería de Catalans il·lustres (see entry).

Plaça de Sant Jaume

From the Plaça de Sant Jaume continue north-west between the Palau de la Generalitat and the Casa dels Canonges (canons' house) to the **cathedral** (see entry) and the Casa de l'Ardiaca (archdeacon's house), now the Institut Municipal d'Història. Opposite, by the Palau Episcopal (bishop's palace, see entry) are towers from the old Roman city wall.

Behind the Palau Episcopal lies the picturesque little Plaça de Sant Felip Neri, with the **Museu de Calçat** (shoe museum); to the north of the bishop's palace, on the far side of the Plaça Nova, stands the modern Architects' Society Building (see entry), famous for its Picasso graffiti.

Plaça de Sant Felip Neri

The Plaça de la Seu (cathedral square) is bounded to the north by the Casa Pia Almoina. Skirt round the north-east side of the cathedral to the Museu Frederic Marès (see entry), then, further on, bear left to the Museu d'Història de la Ciutat (see entry) adjoining the Plaça del Rei (King's Square), the latter flanked by fine old buildings. Return to the Plaça de Sant Jaume or to the Metro station at the Plaça del Angel.

Plaça del Rei

Barri Xino   H–I 8–9

To the south-west of the Barri Gòtic extends a continuation of the old part of the city – the Barri Xino (**Chinese Quarter**). With its maze of narrow streets and alleyways this part of the city is to a large extent in

Location
Between the
Ramblas and
Paral·lel

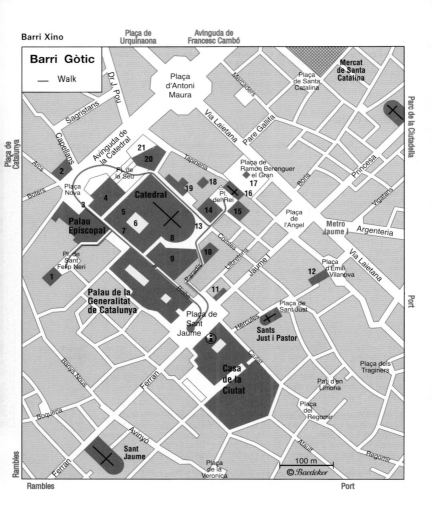

1 Museu del Calçat (Footwear Museum)
2 Architects' Building
3 Towers of Roman city wall
4 Archdeacon's House (Institut Municipal d'Història)
5 Roman Gateway
6 Cathedral Cloister
7 Porta de Santa Eulària
8 Porta de la Pietat (entrance to cloister)
9 Canons' House
10 Pillars of Temple of Augustus (inside)
11 Museu d'Holografia
12 Galería de Catalana Il.lustres
13 Porta de Sant Iu
14 Palau de Llochtinent (Archive of the Crown of Aragón)
15 Palau Clariana Padellás (Museu d'Història de la Ciutat)
16 Capella de Santa Agata
17 Equestrian statue of Ramon Berenguer the Great
18 Saló de Tinell
19 Museu Frederic Marès
20 Casa Pia Almoina
21 Roman city walls

urgent need of redevelopment and is a centre for prostitution, drug trafficking and petty crime and, after dark at least, should be avoided.

See entry — Biblioteca de Catalunya

See entry — Hospital de la Santa Creu

See entry — Sant Pau del Camp

Biblioteca de Catalunya   H 9

The Biblioteca de Catalunya is housed in one part of the former Hospital de la Santa Creu. The library, founded in 1914, today contains around a million volumes as well as a special section on the works of Miguel Cervantes Saavedra, the author of "Don Quixote".

Proceeding from the Carrer del Carme, the visitor turns right and comes to a gateway. The large colourful picture tiles, depicting scenes from the life of St Paul, are worthy of note. There are also brightly coloured tiled decorations in the inner courtyard (with its two-storey arcades and a statue of St Paul from the 17th c.) and on the staircase. The reading room is only open to registered users.

This group of buildings also houses the **Biblioteca Infantil Santa Creu** (children's library) and the **Biblioteca Popular Sant Pau** (public library) as well as part of the University Library.

Location
Carrer del Carme

Metro
Liceu (L3)

Botanical Garden   H 5

Behind the Palau Nacional (see entry) and forming part of the park of Montjuïc (see entry) extends the Botanical Garden (Catalan: **Jardí Botànic**) with its beautiful flora. It was laid out immediately after the World Exhibition of 1929 on a site which included an abandoned quarry, and by virtue of this location it possesses a range of microclimatic zones that can even offer good conditions of growth to exotic plants. Otherwise the stocks of plants are mainly arranged according to geographical categories. The garden is one of the most important examples of its type in Spain.

Close by is the sports area, greatly extended for the 1992 Olympic Games (see Olympic Stadium). On a concrete bridge spanning the Botanical Garden stands the bronze statue of a man bearing the Olympic torch. It commemorates the left-wing educationalist Francesc Ferrer i Guardia (1859–1909), founder of the dissident movement known as the "Escola Moderna". Accused of orchestrating the 1909 riots that ended in bloodshed, he was sentenced to death and executed in Alella near Barcelona.

The gardens are linked to the **Institut Botànic** (Botanical Institute) opposite (specialist visitors only). These gardens are under restoration.

Location
Montjuïc

Metro
Plaça d'Espanya (L1, L3)

Bus
61 (from Plaça Espanya)

★Casa Batlló   G 9–10

The Casa Batlló, situated at the crossroads of the Passeig de Gràcia and the Carrer Aragó, was designed by Antoni Gaudí for the textile manufacturer Josep Batlló i Casanovas and counts as one of the most-famous buildings of the Modernisme school.

The appearance of the façade is characterised by an ornamental structure which seems to have departed completely from any received prin-

Location
Passeig de Gràcia 43

Metro
Gràcia (L2, L3, L4)

ciples of architecture. The window frontage on the first floor is bordered by freely swinging shapes, some of which suggest plants, others entrances to caves. Above that the façade is covered with glazed ceramic tiles in green, blue and ochre colours. The small balconies have railings made out of beaten steel. The wave-shaped roof has, like that of the Casa Milà (see entry), a large number of richly decorated chimneys. Parts of the interior fittings, which were likewise designed by Gaudí, can be seen in the Museu Gaudí (see Parc Güell).

In order to view the interior of the Casa Batlló (at present partially undergoing reconstruction), it is necessary to obtain permission from the Càtedra Gaudí (see Practical Information).

On the left of the Casa Batlló protrudes the **Casa Ametller** (1900), a house built by Josep Puig i Cadafalch in Neo-Gothic style, and at the south-eastern end of the street intersection (the crossing with the Carrer Consell de Cent) stands the **Casa Lleó Morera** (1905; recently restored and now the premises of the Patronat de Turisme de Barcelona), the work of Lluís Domènech i Montaner. Because of the unconventional and totally distinctive character of each of the three buildings, the group is referred to as the "mansana de la discòrdia" ("apple of discord"), where the play on words depends on the double meaning of the word "mansana" ("block of houses" as well as "apple").

Casa Calvet   H 10

The Casa Calvet (1898–1900), not far north of the Plaça de Catalunya, was also designed by Antoni Gaudí. Compared to his other work it is spartan in the meagre decoration of the façade. For this building Gaudí was awarded the architectural prize of the City of Barcelona.

The furnishings, some of which are also by Gaudí, can be seen in the Museu Gaudí (see Parc Güell); the interior of the Casa Calvet is not open to the public, as the building is privately owned.

Location
Carrer Casp 48

Metro
Urquinaona
(L1, L4)

Casa de Caritat   H 9

The Casa de Caritat is situated in the old area of the city to the south of the Plaça de Catalunya. Since the 13th c. the area has belonged to the Augustinian canons and later a seminary was set up there. The cloister acquired its present appearance, which follows Tuscan models, in the middle of the 18th c. Today the Casa de Caritat has been enlarged by a modern extension and serves as a cultural centre and exhibition hall.

In 1966 a modern exhibition hall, white, with vast areas of glass on its main façade, was completed south-east of the Casa de Caritat. It houses the **Museu d'Art Contemporani**, lack of space preventing the collections from being displayed in the Museu d'Art Modern (see entries).

In front of the museum is the Plaça des Angels, likewise recently given a new look. Here stands the former convent of the same name which was erected in 1560 in a late Gothic style. At the present time it is undergoing conversion for use as a central library for the City Museum.

Location
Carrer Montalegre

Metro
Catalunya (L1, L3),
Universitat (L1, L2)

Plaça des Angels

Casa de la Ciutat   I 10

On the south-east side of the Plaça de Sant Jaume, which forms the centre of the Barri Gòtic (see entry), stands the Casa de la Ciutat (**City Hall**). This magnificent building, which dates originally from the 14th c.,

Location
Plaça de Sant Jaume

◀ *The Casa Batlló*

Casa Milà

Metro
Liceu (L3),
Jaume I (L4)

possesses side façades which are still in part Gothic, whilst the main façade was rebuilt in 1847 by Josep Mas in the Classical style. The inner courtyard with its beautiful flight of steps is worth seeing.

Inside the City Hall is the great Saló de Cent (council chamber; 14th c.) with wall hangings in the Catalan colours of red and yellow. There is also the Saló de les Cròniques with its marble flooring by Josep Maria Sert.

Casa de l'Ardiaca

See Institut Municipal d'Història

Casa Lleó Morera

See Casa Batlló

★★Casa Milà   F 10

Location
Passeig de
Gràcia 92

Metro
Diagonal (L3, L5)

The Casa Milà, situated on a corner site at the crossing of the Passeig de Gràcia with the Carrer de Provença, is the last and most-famous secular building of Antoni Gaudí. In the design of this multi-storey dwelling block he departed completely from established principles of construction, so that the result resembles a piece of sculpture rather than a functional building. The observer will search in vain for absolute straight lines; instead the façade of carved natural stone displays rounded windows, metal balcony railings twining around in plant-like shapes, and a curved roof line on which the many chimneys confer a formal rather than a functional character.

Casa Milà in the Passeig de Gràcia

The complete building is grouped around two oval-shaped air wells. Even when it was being erected the building aroused passionate controversy: serious differences arose between Gaudí and his client Milà i Camps-Segimon on account of the long construction period and the alterations which Gaudí continually kept putting off making. It was also not long before the building acquired the derisive nickname of **"Pedrera"** (quarry).

Recently the façade was thoroughly cleaned and the rest of the building is at present being restored. On the ground floor there are offices of the Caixa de Catalunya, which is responsible for the conservation of the building, and some shops. The interior of the Casa Milà is not open to the general public, but there are guided tours of the roof (advance booking recommended; for information tel. 934845995). The entrance is on the Carrer de Procença, from which the inner courtyard is reached through a remarkable wrought-iron gate. A narrow staircase leads up to the roof truss. Its load-bearing construction of narrow tiled ribs running in vertical parallel arches bears witness to Gaudí's genius as a structural engineer.

The roof area itself is then reached, with its strangely shaped chimneys partly covered in mosaics. A walk around up here also rewards the visitor with beautiful views across the city (the Sagrada Família in the distance to the north-east).

Casa-Museu Verdaguer   outside the city plan

The Vil·la Joana, which has been converted into a museum for the Catalan poet Jacint Verdaguer, is situated in the north-west outskirts of the city in the district of Vallvidrera at the southern foot of Mt Tibidabo. It is best reached by taking the train from the Plaça de Catalunya (see entry) in the direction of Sant Cugat (FGC) as far as the station Baixador de Vallvidrera; from here the museum is reached after a five-minute walk in a south-easterly direction.

Location
Vil·la Joana
(Vallvidrera)

Railway
(FGC)
Baixador de
Vallvidrera

The **villa** was originally a manor house, partly dating back to the Middle Ages. Its owners gave the ailing Verdaguer shelter here. After a few weeks the poet died on the June 10th 1902 at the age of 57.

Open Tue.–Sun.
10am–2pm

The **museum** partly occupies rooms used by Verdaguer and subsequently kept virtually unaltered, and displays original manuscripts as well as contemporary paintings and drawings. A large part is devoted to Verdaguer's epic poem "L'Atlàntida", for which the painter F. Vall Verdaguer has painted a series of oil pictures. A visual and aural commentary completes the overview of Verdaguer's life and work.

In a pine wood nearby is the **"Font Vella"** (old spring).

Casa Vicens   E 10

The Casa Vicens, situated in a narrow side street off the Carrer Gran de Gràcia, was built by Gaudí between 1883 and 1888 for the ceramics manufacturer Manuel Vicens i Montaner and is one of the earliest of the architect's designs to be realised.

Location
Carrer Carolines
24

Metro
Lesseps (L3)

The still largely linear conception shows the strong influence of the Moorish-Spanish architectural tradition, and this impression is strengthened by the generous use of tiled decoration. The property is separated from the street by a metal fence consisting of stylised fan palm leaves.

The **interior** of the Casa Vicens is not open to the public.

Detail of the ornamental ironwork of the Casa Vicens

A model of the Sagrada Família in Catalunya en Miniatura

★Catalunya en Miniatura

The model exposition Catalunya en Miniatura (**Catalonia in Miniature**) is situated 17 km (11 mi.) south-west of the city centre in Torrelles de Llobregat, best reached by car via the Martorell road, turning off at Molins del Rei for Vincenç dels Horts. Buses are fairly infrequent so anyone relying on public transport should consider a taxi for the return journey.

The exposition includes models (scale 1:25) of all the most-important but also some of the less well-known monuments and buildings in Catalonia, as well as modern transport and industrial layouts. Many of the model trains, cars and ships can be coin operated. There are kiosks providing refreshments and a restaurant near the entrance.

Excursion
Torrelles de
Llobregat
17 km (11 mi.) SW

Bus
Line TISA,
about every hour

★★Cathedral   I 10

On Mont Tabor, which at 12 m (40 ft) is the highest point in the Barri Gòtic (see entry), stands the cathedral (Santa Creu or Santa Eulàlia). It was begun in 1298 on the site of a Romanesque building, of which a few stone reliefs are still preserved at the north-east doorway. By 1448 it was completed except for the main façade and the dome, which were added in 1898 and 1913.

Location
Plaça de la Seu

Metro
Jaume I (L4)

Open daily
8am–1.30pm,
4–7.30pm

The orientation of the cathedral is rather unusual: the apse and altar area lie to the south-east whilst the main façade faces north-west.

Coming from the Plaça Sant Jaume, the visitor arrives at the very beautiful **cloister** (Claustre) with its magnolias and palms. It is entered by the Portal de Santa Eulàlia. The cloister dates from 1380–1451 and is lined with numerous chapels containing the altars of various saints. Of note is the fountain which is crowned by a small statue of St George (Sant Jordi) with the dragon. At Corpus Christi there is a custom of blowing an egg and letting it spin on the fountain. There is a special explanation for the geese that inhabit the cloister: in the Middle Ages they guarded the cathedral and its treasures, for their aggressiveness and vociferousness have been well known since the averted storming of the Roman Capitol (387 BC), and this tradition lives on today.

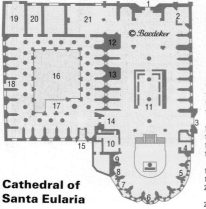

Cathedral of Santa Eularia

1 Main entrance
2 Baptistery
3 Porta de Sant Iu
4 Capella de les Sants Innocents
5 Capella de l'Aparició
6 Capella de Santo Cristo
7 Capella del Patrocini
8 Capella de Sant Miquel
9 Capella de Sant Antoni
10 Sacristy
11 Choirstalls
12 Capella de Sant Climent
13 Capella de Sant Raymund de Penyafort
14 Porta de Sant Serveri
15 Pora de la Pietat
16 Claustre (cloister)
17 Font de Sant Jordi (St George's Well)
18 Porta de Sant Eulària
19 Capella de Santa Llúcia
20 Sala Capitular (Chapter House)
21 Capella de Santisim

In the south-western corner of the cloister is the Capella de Santa Llucia, founded in 1270, and next to it the museum.

The cathedral **museum** (Museu de la Catedral) in the former chapter house (Sala Capitular) displays paintings by Spanish masters from the 15th and 16th c., sculptures, and liturgical articles. Open daily 11am–1pm.

The High Gothic **interior** (83.3 m (273 ft) long, 37.2 m (122 ft) wide, 25.5 m (84 ft) high) is divided into three aisles. The main aisle and side aisles of the cathedral are approximately the same height. High up there is a row of small windows. On the side aisles underneath the low galleries are chapels, mainly from the 16th and 17th c. and with ornate Baroque altars. The most impressive is the Capilla del Santíssim Sagrament, which is to be found on the left of the high altar. It is the former chapter house and contains the 15th/16th c. alabaster tombstone of Bishop Olegarius (d. 1136) and the "Lepanto Christ", allegedly the figurehead of the flagship of Don Juan of Austria (see Museu Marítim) in which he defeated the Turks in 1571. In the last side chapel before the left transept there is a black madonna which resembles the famous image of Maria in Montserrat (see entry).

The magnificent **stained-glass windows** are mainly 15th c. Also of interest are the choir stalls (15th c.), which stand in the middle of the main aisle and are enclosed on three sides, and the beautiful pulpit of 1403. In the Capilla Major there is a Late Gothic retable (reredos; 16th c.).

From the Capilla Major a staircase leads down to the **crypt**. Illuminated by hosts of candles it contains the alabaster sarcophagus of the patron saint of the city and the cathedral, Santa Eulàlia, an Italian work dating from 1330.

In the sacristy the **cathedral treasury** (Catalan, tresor), which includes gold and silver articles and an alabaster image of the Madonna and rosary, is worth seeing.

From the **south-west tower** of the cathedral (210 steps; access from inside the building) there is a very rewarding view of the city, its hinterland and the sea.

See Institut Municipal d'Història   Casa de l'Ardiaca

See entry   Palau Episcopal

Centre Permanent d'Artesania   G 10

In recent years Barcelona has developed into a notable design centre. The Centre Permanent d'Artesania has in three rooms exhibitions and displays on various topics and themes (open during shop hours).

Location
Passeig de
Gràcia 55

Metro
Gràcia (L3, L4)

As a result of European regions having gained more importance, close cooperation has also existed with the Rhône-Alpes area of France and Baden-Württemberg in Germany, especially with the Stuttgart provincial inspectorate.

Col·legi d'Arquitectes

See Architects' Society Building

◀ *The north-west main façade of the cathedral*

Col·legi de les Teresianes   D 7

Location
Carrer Ganduxer
95–105

Railway station
(FGC)
Bonanova

The Col·legi de les Tere-
sianes is the parent con-
vent of the sisterhood of
Teresa, which takes its
name from St Teresa of
Avila (1515–82).

The building of the col-
lege had already been
started when in 1888 Antoni
Gaudí was commissioned
to complete it.

Measured against other
works by this architect the
Col·legi de les Teresianes is
unwonted sobriety – indeed
a concession to the rule of
the order.

The brick-built pointed
arches of the façade, particularly on the top storey,
point to Gothic models.

The buildings house a
school and therefore access
to the public is limited.

★Colonia Güell   outside the city plan

Location
Santa Coloma del
Cervelló

Railway station
(FGC)
Molí Nou

Open Mon.–Fri.
10.15am–1.15pm,
4–6pm (closed
Thu. pm),
Sun., pub. hols.
10am–1.30pm

Take the FGC from the Plaça d'Espanya as far as Moli Nou (about 20 minutes) then follow the main road northwards to the Recinte Industrial
Güell, situated just on the outskirts of Santa Coloma. The route through
the precinct to the church is signposted only intermittently (sometimes
as "Cripta", sometimes as "Eglesia").

In 1898 Count Eusebi Güell, the great patron of Antoni Gaudí, had a
social settlement, the Colonia Güell, laid out for the workers in his textile factory in Santa Coloma del Cervelló outside Barcelona to the south-
west. Gaudí was commissioned to build a church for the settlement and
his preliminary sketches reveal a startling similarity with the Sagrada
Família (see entry). However the church in the workers' settlement was
actually not built in the same style as the latter.

The lower part of the planned **church**, the so-called "crypt", was constructed between 1908 and 1916 on a pine-clad hill. In its design two
aspects are clearly visible: on the one hand the static and formal structural details of Gothic – in so far as these were adopted by Gaudí – and
on the other hand the principle of "oblique supports" which he introduced, and which, together with parabolic enclosing arches, permits a
spatial design free from all restraints.

The mosaics, especially the one above the main doorway, are particularly noteworthy. The pews in the church were also designed by Gaudí.

Most of the prism-shaped supporting pillars are of columnar basalt;
more can be seen lying in the sparse pine woods in front of the church
where there is also a bust of Antoni Gaudí.

The "Crypt" by Gaudí, on the pine-clad hill of Santa Coloma

Costa Daurada

The term "Costa Daurada" (Spanish Costa Dorada, golden coast) refers to the coastline between the mouth of the River Tordera (which also here forms the border between the provinces of Barcelona and Girona) and the delta of the River Ebre (Spanish Ebro) to the south of Tarragona. This area, which extends along about 260 km (162 mi.) of the Mediterranean coast, is well known for its gently sloping beaches and its fine, golden sand, as well as being valued for its mild climate.

Within the province of Barcelona, Sitges and Vilanova i La Geltrú deserve special mention.

Excursion

About 37 km (23 mi.) to the south-west of Barcelona, Sitges is one of the oldest Spanish coastal resorts. Even nowadays it is less subject to mass tourism than other places and moreover is patronised by a discerning upmarket clientele with cultural demands. Many residents of Barcelona have second homes here. The British writer G.K. Chesterton invented his character Father Brown here.

Sitges

Railway station (RENFE) from Central-Sants or Passeig de Gràia to Sitges (45 min.)

Worth visiting is the **Museu Cau Ferrat** (housed in the former home of the art collector Santiago Rusiñol) with its collection of Modernist art, paintings by Picasso and El Greco and others. Attached to the same building is the **Museu Maricel de Mar** (furniture, glass and ceramics going back as far as the Middle Ages; paintings by Josep Maria Sert).

In a patrician house dating from the late 18th c. is housed the **Museu Romàntic** (furniture and a collection of dolls).

Within the municipality of Sitges are the three sporting harbours of Aiguadolç, Garraf and Port Ginestra.

The **Gran Casino de Barcelona** is located in Sitges.

Vilanova i La Geltrú

A short distance to the south-west of Sitges lies the busy commercial centre of Vilanova i La Geltrú. In the **Castell** (13th c. castle) there is a museum of art. The **Casa Papiol** on the Carrer Major, with its upper-class furnishings, is now a museum open to the public.

Situated close to the railway station is the **museum** named after its founder, the Catalan minister and poet Victor Balaguer (d. 1901) (antiquities; paintings, including an Annunciation by El Greco; a small ethnographic collection).

Near the harbour, on the Carrer Almiral Cervera, is the novel **Museu Curiositats Marineres** with all kinds of oddities connected with the sea.

Drassanes

See Museu Marítim

Eglesia de Betlem   H 9

Location
Rambla dels
Estudis

Metro
Liceu (L3)

At the crossing of the Rambla dels Estudis with the Carrer del Carme is to be seen the Baroque façade of the Eglesia de Betlem, built between 1681 and 1732, formerly a Jesuit church. It is characterised by its heavily embossed stonework. In the entrance portal are portrayed Ignatius of Loyola, the founder of the order, Francesco Borgia, the third general of the Jesuit order, as well as the birth of Christ. The rich Baroque furnishings and decorations inside the church were completely destroyed by fire in 1938; their restoration in unadorned classical forms is artistically of little significance.

Palau Moja

Opposite the side façade of the church and on the other side of the Rambla stands the Palau Moja, a palace which has reverted to its Baroque origins.

Eglesia de la Concepció   F 9

Location
Rambla de
Catalunya

Metro
Diagonal (L3, L5)

One would never expect to find a Gothic church here in this extension of the city which was laid out after 1860 and in fact the Eglesia de la Concepció (Church of the Conception) was built in 1293 in the Barri Gòtic (see entry). Between 1871 and 1888 it was dismantled stone by stone and transported to its present location. The interior is flanked by chapels; the attractive cloister dates from the 14th c.

★★Eixample

The extension of the city into the Eixample district coincided with the development of Modernisme (see Baedeker Special p. 30). This style of art and architecture, associated above all with Barcelona, embraces every variation from late Historicism through to Art Nouveau and does so without undergoing the complete cultural break that, for instance occurred in Germany between the period of rapid industrial expansion and the later period.

The new city area particularly attracted circles of rich upper-class people, and architects like Antoni Gaudí, Lluís Domènech i Montaner and Josep Puig i Cadafalch, with their magnificent buildings, conferred on the Eixample its unmistakable charm.

Also relevant is the fact that Spain was neutral in both world wars, while the Civil War (1936–39) was far from being able to inflict the same

A Model of Town Planning

Despite the phonetic similarity the name "Eixample" has nothing at all to do with the English word "example" but means "extension" or "expansion". Even so, the Eixample does represent, even today, an exemplary piece of modern town planning.

The district extends in an arc around the old part of the city (Barri Gòtic and Barri Xino) out as far as the foothills of Tibidabo and Carmel. It is instantly recognisable by its rectilinear network of streets running between the equally charactaristic "mansanas" (residential blocks) with their cut off corners.

Until the mid-19th c. Barcelona's boundaries stood at the limits of the then still partially walled old quarter, beyond which undeveloped land extended out to what at the time were neighbouring localities. The revocation of Catalan privileges by Philip V (1714) and subsequent forfeiture of the city's position of pre-eminence in the Mediterranean, precipitated a period of economic decline precluding any possibility of growth.

This changed with the reawakening of the Catalan national consciousness, which in 1814 led to the "Renaixença" (rebirth) when, in the wake of the Romantic movement and influenced by the Wars of Liberation of the time, there emerged in regions all over Europe a new awareness of their history and culture. At the same time the growth of industry initiated an era of upper-class prosperity, the effect of which was soon felt by the city. In 1860 the ancient city walls were finally torn down and Barcelona's urban area began to expand at an astonishing rate, due in part to the incorporation of several outlying communities.

When the expansion of the city was just beginning, controversy broke out among town planners as to what would be the best design, one which would be up to date but at the same time practical. The various suggestions were finally reduced to two: a proposal by the architect Antoni Rovira i Trias for a network of streets radiating out from the Old Town; and a chequerboard plan by Ildefons Cerdà. The technical commission charged with making the decision opted initially in 1859 for Rovira's scheme; but by a royal decree of May 31st 1860 the "Pla Cerdà" was adopted.

Ildefons Cerdà's great achievement lay in creating a scheme that, from the start, made it possible to resist haphazard new development, demanding adherence to a plan in the true sense of the word. The aim was to create a large-scale urban environment permeated by light and air. The chequerboard layout with its, even by today's standards, generously proportioned streets and large (100 × 100 m (328 × 328 ft)) residential blocks, was intended to allow any destination within the new city to be reached in the shortest possible time. Thus it was that two magnificent boulevards were included, transecting the area diagonally – the Avinguda de la Diagonal and the Avinguda de la Meridiana (the latter running parallel to the Greenwich Meridian at longitude 2°10'E), forming the Plaça de les Glòries Catalanes at their intersection. While the Diagonal has been completed along almost its entire intended length from the Zona Universitaria in the west to the sea in the east, the final section of the Meridiana between Glòries Catalanes and Ciutadella was never finished.

The original lithograph of the design for the city extension is on display in the Museu d'Història de la Ciutat (see entry).

kind of damage as the bombing campaigns to which other European countries were subjected from 1939 to 1945.

Most of the best examples of buildings of the Modernisme period are to be found in the **Quadrat d'Or** (see entry), the area on either side of the Passeig de Gràcia between the Plaça de Catalunya and the Avinguda de la Diagonal.

Exhibition Grounds   H 5–6

Location
Avinguda Reina
Maria Cristina

Metro
Plaça d'Espanya
(L1, L3)

The Exhibition Grounds (**Fira de Barcelona**) extend across all the land between the Plaça d'Espanya (see entry) and the steps leading up to the Palau Nacional (see entry). The area is bisected by the Avinguda de la Reina Maria Cristina which is bordered by fountains illuminated after dark.

Barcelona is the most important trade fair centre of the country, even outranking Madrid, and comparable with those in other countries. At present there are about 40 large international events held annually.

For information about the Barcelona Fair and other regular events contact the tourist office (see Practical Information, Information).

Exhibition Grounds
(Fira de Barcelona)

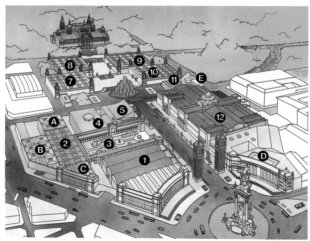

1	Palacio de las Comunicaciones	9/10	Palacio de Victoria Eugenia
2	Palacio del Cincuentenasio	11	Pabellón INI
3	Palacio del Universo	12	Palacio de la Metallurgía
4	Palacio Ferial		
5	Palacio de Congresos	A–D	Extensions
7/8	Palacio de Alfonso XIII	E	Pabellón van der Rohe

The Dragon Gate of the Finca Güell ▶

★Finca Güell   D 4

Location
Avinguda
Pedralbes 7

Metro
Palau Reial, Maria
Cristina (L3)

The Finca Güell, built 1884–87 by Antoni Gaudí for the Count Güell as a country residence outside what was then the built-up area of the city, today lies in the district of Pedralbes, one of Barcelona's most select residential areas, in the immediate vicinity of the Palau de Pedralbes. The property consists of three buildings: the single storey lodge to the left of the entrance, the large former stables and, attached to them, the round riding hall.

From a stylistic point of view the group of buildings is closely linked to the Casa Vicens (1883–88, see entry) and, in common with that building, is reminiscent of the architecture of the Spanish Moorish period.

Exterior The roofs of both the lodge and the riding hall are spanned by domes crowned with lanterns; the façades are covered in decorative tiles to which the window sections, executed in clinker brick, make an attractive contrast. Worthy of note are the elaborate openwork brick ledges which surround the roof of the stables.

Especially impressive is the wrought-iron, 5-m (16-ft) wide entrance gate that gets its name **Dragon Gate** from its main motif. It demonstrates particularly clearly the influences of Art Nouveau on the work of Gaudí.

The **interior** of the Finca today houses the Càtedra Gaudí, an institute dedicated to the maintenance and preservation of the work of Antoni Gaudí, and from where permission to view some of these buildings can be obtained (see Practical Information, Information). Apart from this the estate is not open to the public.

The Fundació Antoni Tàpies

Fira de Barcelona

See Exhibition Grounds

★Fundació Antoni Tàpies   G 9

On the Carrer Aragó, not far to the south-west of where it crosses the Passeig de Gràcia, is the brick building built 1880–85 by Lluís Domènech i Montaner that used to be the premises of the publishing house of Montaner i Simon. Since 1984 it has been occupied by the Fundació Antoni Tàpies, a foundation established by this Barcelona artist who was born in the city in 1923. On the roof there is a surreal sculpture made of metal wires and bands.

Location
Carrer Aragó 255

Metro
Passeig de Gràcia
(L2, L3, L4)

Open Tue.–Sun.
11am–8pm

The **interior** of the building has been emptied as far as possible in order to make space for exhibitions. On the main level slightly below the entrance are temporary exhibitions while one level lower is the permanent exhibition which comprises a selection of Antoni Tàpies' graphic works. The gallery, supported by decorative cast-iron pillars and leaving the middle of the building clear rather in the manner of a Roman atrium, is occupied by the well-stocked specialist library devoted to 20th c. art and Asian culture. The foundation possesses the most comprehensive collection of the artist's works and has taken on the role of a research centre for contemporary art.

★★Fundació Joan Miró   I 6

The Fundació Joan Miró nestles in parkland on the north side of Montjuïc (see entry). It was here that the architects Josep Lluís Sert and Jaume Freixa erected a purpose-built home for the foundation established in 1971 by Joan Miró. The building, which was officially opened in 1988, is constructed in white concrete and comprises rigidly cubic elements, which on the inside are lit up by semicircular skylights. There are two inner courtyards.

Location
Avinguda de
Miramar
(Montjuïc)

Bus
61, then the
Funicular de
Montjuïc

On the left of the entrance level, behind the ticket office, are the rooms reserved for temporary exhibitions of contemporary art, whilst the permanent exhibition occupies the right-hand part of the ground floor and the whole of the upper storey. The museum's exhibits comprise about 5000 items.

Open Tue.–Sat.
10am–8pm
(Jul.–Sep.
10am–8pm), Thu.
11am.–9.30pm,
Sun., pub. hols.
10.30am–2.30pm

A **tour** of the Miró collection begins to the right of the first inner courtyard. Here there is first of all a chronological overview of the artist's life and work (examples of his work in reproduction form; model of the Spanish pavilion for the Paris World Exhibition of 1937) and also an enormous, brilliantly coloured wall tapestry. In the next passageway there is an original mercury fountain ("Font de Mercuri") by Alexander Calder. Then follows the plastic design for a group of figures in the Paris district of La Défense (in a coloured man-made substance) and after that a room with numerous monochrome graphics.

A staircase leads to the upper floor. Here can be seen an extensive collection of paintings and there is a good view from above over the previously mentioned group of figures and the wall tapestry. In front of the entrance to the roof terrace (with its excellent view over the city and its coloured statues) stands the great marble "sun-bird"; this is followed by a series of original copper printing plates belonging to the "Mallorca" series. In the octagon are many small-scale graphics (starting in 1901 and displayed in choronological order clockwise). The collection is

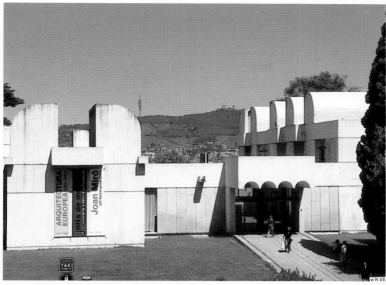

A view of Tibidabo from the Fundació Joan Miro

completed by some works by Miró's contemporaries (several Catalans, Alexander Calder, Max Ernst, Henry Moore).

In the upper part of the building is a library; a cafeteria and also a kiosk selling books and prints are located on the ground floor.

Gabinet de Física Experimental   A 9

The Gabinet de Física Experimental "Mentora Alsina" is on the road from Vallvidrera to Tibidabo (see entry), close to the lower station of the beach funicular which goes up the mountain.

The museum has its origins in the former private collection of Ferran Alsina i Perellada, who occupied the house until 1907, and it now belongs to the city of Barcelona. It has on display working models and originals of machines and instruments from the fields of mechanics, optics, acoustics, thermodynamics and electricity.

Location
Carretera
Vallvidrera-
Tibidabo

Open by
arrangement

Gabinet Numismàtic   H–I 9

The Gabinet Numismàtic de Catalunya (**Gallery of Coins**) is housed in the Palau de la Virreina (see entry) on the Ramblas. The collection forms part of the Museu Nacional d'Art de Catalunya (see Palau Nacional).

The museum's exhibits are derived from various private collections which since 1902 have come into the hands of the city either as gifts, bequests or loans. The collection numbers more than 10,000 items: medals, coins, banknotes and stocks and shares, mainly from Catalonia

Location
Rambla 99

Metro
Liceu (L3)

Open by
arrangement

◀ *The "Font de Mercuri" in the Fundació Joan Miró*

and going back to the 5th c. BC. Of particular significance are the mintings from the Greek colony Emporion (Empúries) and Iberic, West Gothic and Roman coins, as well as coins from Latin America.

Gabinet Postal

See Palau de la Virreina

Galeria de Catalans il·lustres   I 10

Location
Carrer del Bisbe
Caçador 3

Metro
Jaume I (L4)

**Open by
arrangement,**
tel. 933151111

The Galeria de Catalans il·lustres (**Gallery of Famous Catalans**; part of the Museu d'Història de la Ciutat) is situated in the Barri Gòtic (see entry), only a few steps south of the Plaça de l'Angel and the metro station Jaume I. The building, the Gothic Palau Requesens, stands right on the Roman city wall and is at the same time the seat of the Acadèmia de Bones Lletres de Barcelona (Academy of Humanities).

The **collection** has some fifty portraits of Catalans who have made a contribution to literature, art, science and religion as well as in military affairs. Each portrait has a biographical overview with it.

Gran Casino de Barcelona

See Costa Daurada, Sitges

Gran Teatre del Liceu

See Liceu

Hospital de la Santa Creu   H 8–9

Location
Carrer del
Hospital

Metro
Liceu (L3)

In the middle of the Barri Xino (see entry), behind the market hall (see Mercat de Sant Josep), is the large complex of buildings, grouped around a cloistered courtyard, of the old Hospital de la Santa Creu (Holy Cross Hospital; **Antic Hospital**). It was founded in 1401 and not completed until the 17th c., which explains the varying architectural styles.

From the Carrer del Hospital the building is entered by a pair of 16th c. doors, on the right-hand side of which stands the chapel. In the middle of the **cloister** there is a Baroque cross with a curved shaft, behind which is a large arch with a beautiful staircase. In the opposite building is housed a branch of the university library, while in the wings adjoining the Carrer del Carme the Biblioteca de Catalunya (see entry) is located.

At the start of the 20th c. it became evident that the rooms of the Antic Hospital no longer answered its needs. The architect Lluís Domènech i Montaner was therefore commissioned to build a new up-to-date building in the Eixample district (see entry), the Hospital de la Santa Creu i de Sant Pau (see below).

Hospital de la Santa Creu i de Sant Pau   E–F 13–14

Location
Carrer Sant Antoni
Maria Claret

At the beginning of the 20th c. the Hospital de la Santa Creu i de Sant Pau took over what had been up to then the role of the ancient Hospital de la Santa Creu (see above). To the north of the Sagrada Família (see

The façade of the Hospital de la Santa Creu i de Sant Pau

entry), with which the site of the hospital is connected by the broad Avinguda de Gaudí, the architect Lluís Domènech i Montaner built a hospital complex which, in contradiction to established principles of construction, was not a unified single large building but combined on one single large site the various hospital departments, each housed in a pavilion and separated from the others by large expanses of grass.

Metro
Hospital de Sant
Pau (L5)

The **façades** of the buildings are decorated in a fashion characteristic of Modernisme with a mixture of brick-faced masonry, colourful ceramics and natural stone.

Institut Municipal d'Història   I 10

The Institut Municipal d'Història (**City History Institute**), founded in 1922, is housed in the beautiful **Casa de l'Ardiaca** (Archdeacon's House), part of which go back to the 12th c. and which essentially acquired the external appearance which it has today in the 15th c., during the Late Gothic period, whilst the decorative figures show the influence of the Italian Renaissance.

Location
Carrer Santa
Llúcia 1

Metro
Jaume I (L4)

The interior of the building is only open to academics; of note however is the **inner courtyard**, surrounded by arcades, with multi-coloured decorative tiles and a Gothic fountain.

Jardí Botànic

See Botanical Garden

Jardins Mossèn Costa i Llobera

See Montjuïc

Jardins Mossèn Jacint Verdaguer

See Montjuïc

Liceu   I 9

Location
Rambla dels
Caputxins 65

Metro
Liceu (L3)

The Gran Teatre del Liceu is the largest opera house in Spain and next to La Scala Milan the second largest traditional theatre in Europe. Built in 1844 and inaugurated in 1848 it conceals behind its somewhat plain façade a magnificent auditorium.

In January 1994 the building was almost completely destroyed by fire; the restored theatre's reopening is planned for autumn 1999.

Llotja

See Stock Exchange

Marinemuseum

See Museu Marítim

Mercat del Born   I 11

Location
Carrer del Comerç

Metro
Barceloneta (L4)

A short distance to the south-west of the Parc de la Ciutadella (see entry) and on the far side of the Passeig de Picasso stands the Mercat del Born, once the largest market hall in the city. It was built 1873–76 on a steel frame from designs by the architects Antoni Rovira, Josep Fontserè and Josep Comet.

Today the hall is used as a cultural centre with regular functions and temporary exhibitions.

Mercat de Sant Antoni   H 7

Location
Ronda de Sant
Pau/Ronda de
Sant Antoni

Metro
Universitat (L1),
Paral·lel (L3);
Sant Antoni (L2)

The Mercat de Sant Antoni at the south-western edge of the Barri Xino (see entry) is one of the largest market halls in Barcelona still in active use. The steel-frame building (1872–82) by Antoni Rovira i Trias occupies the area of a complete block of streets and the market offers an extremely large choice of fruit, vegetables, fish and seafood.

Around the outside of the building are stalls selling textiles, books, records, coins and stamps.

★Mercat de Sant Josep   I 9

Location
Rambla de Sant
Josep

On the south-west side of the Rambla dels Flors (Rambla de Sant Josep; see Ramblas), where in the morning the colourful flower market is held, and directly next to the Palau de la Virreina (see entry), is the large

Phoenix from the Ashes

Barcelona's opera house stands on what was once sacred ground, site of a monastery belonging to the barefoot Trinitarians, which burned down in 1835. The modernisation of the city centre taking place at that time – to which other conventual buildings located in the Ramblas also had to give way – saw the establishment of an open square.

Architect Miquel Garriga i Roca's "Liceo Filarmónica Dramatico Barcelonés de Su Majestad la Reina Isabel" as the opera house was officially and somewhat elaborately christened, was for all that a bourgeois creation. The Barcelonan love of music is deep rooted: in 1813 Rossini's opera "The Italian Girl in Algiers" evoked a certain enthusiasm for Italian opera, setting the tone for several decades. The upper middle class, who from the mid-century onwards became ever more prosperous, made the Liceu their own, a meeting place with which they could identify and at that time unrivalled in size and splendour throughout Europe or indeed the world.

Barely a dozen years had passed however when catastrophe struck for the first time on April 9th 1861, fire ravaging the building including the foundations and façade. The opera-loving citizens of Barcelona rallied round, neither effort nor expense being spared; a year later the Liceu was fully restored, more splendid and imposing than ever. Josep Oriol Mestres' relatively plain façade concealed a luxuriously appointed auditorium, richly embellished with Neo-Pompeiian wall and ceiling paintings to which the finest exponents of 19th c. Catalan Realism, indebted to the style of the French Deuxième Empire, contributed.

As the end of the 19th c. drew closer and closer, so public interest in music from other parts of Europe grew and grew; the Liceu became a leading Wagnerian venue, while at the same time acting more and more as a focal point for the cultured upper middle class. Not just somewhere to enjoy opera and music, the Liceu was now *the* place to be seen. The world's most celebrated soloists regularly performed on its stage. Since those days many of the boxes have remained in private hands, passed down from generation to generation within the same family (which can sometimes make it difficult to obtain tickets on the open market).

Then in January 1994 the disaster of 1861 was repeated. Fire broke out during preparations for a performance of Paul Hindemith's "Mathis der Maler", and the whole interior of the Liceu was again destroyed. Not only was the material damage enormous, the loss felt by music lovers was perhaps greater still. But once again the response was swift: even before the rubble had ceased smoldering, Jordi Pujol, Catalan head of government, pledged that the opera house would be speedily rebuilt. A solidarity fund set up spontaneously by the soprano Montserrat Caballé attracted support from a host of world-famous artists. Where previously it was the prosperous upper middle class who rallied round to provide generous patronage, today it is chiefly local and regional businesses across the financial, industrial and service sectors. Meanwhile the Liceu has not only been rebuilt, but also considerably enlarged, incorporating the latest technology. It is to reopen with a gala performance of Puccini's "Turandot" in the autumn of 1999.

Crustaceans in the Mercat de Sant Josep

Metro
Liceu (L3)

Mercat de Sant Josep (also called the Mercat de la Boqueria), the oldest and most important market hall in Barcelona and the one which is most worth visiting.

It was opened in 1840 and offers an impressive and colourful range of goods including fruit, vegetables, meat, regional sausages. In the centre of the hall is the fish market. At other stalls snacks can be obtained.

Pla de l'Os

Opening out in front of the market hall is the Pla de l'Os, which forms part of the Rambles. The name means "Bear Square" and even today travellers occasionally can be seen with their dancing bears. In the street paving is a ground mosaic (1976) by Joan Miró. Opposite lies a rather irreverently flamboyant building with an umbrella and a large Chinese dragon forming part of the façade.

★★Montjuïc   H 3–J 7

Location
SW of the Old Town

Metro Paral·lel (L3);
continue by
funicular and
cable car

On the southern side of the city and sloping steeply down to the sea rises Montjuïc (213 m (700 ft)). Crowned by a fortress built on its summit, it is the most extensive and most frequented recreational area within the city boundaries and repays an extended visit not just for its scenic beauty with its rich vegetation and large parks, but also because of its museums and amusement park.

From the port (see entry) the visitor can travel by ★★**cable car** (Transbordador Aerí) to the Parc de Miramar, about halfway up the north-eastern side of the hill.

From the Avinguda del Paral·lel, which connects the port with the Plaça d'Espanya (see entry), next to the Paral·lel metro station, there is a beach **cable railway**, running initially underground, up to the Avinguda de

The Castell de Montjuïc

Miramar, which runs halfway up the side of Montjuïc. Near the upper station is the large municipal open-air swimming pool.

A chairlift (operating Jun.–Sep. Mon.–Fri. noon–8.30pm, Sat., Sun. and public holidays 11am–2.45pm, 4–7.30pm; Sep.–Jun., except Christmas holidays, daily 11am–2.45pm, 4.30–7pm) provides a continuation up to the castle and offers visitors an even better view, especially across the harbour basin, which is, as already mentioned, spanned by the cable railway. From the intermediate station the visitor can reach the amusement park directly. The chairlift ends immediately next to the castle at the top and there is a restaurant which enjoys an excellent vantage point.

Castell de Montjuïc

The whole of the summit area of Montjuïc is occupied by the extensive buildings and grounds which make up the Castell de Montjuïc (fortress). From the corner bastions in particular, the visitor has a panoramic view across the whole of the metropolis. On the west side stands an ornate memorial to Francisco Franco, which is gradually becoming dilapidated and in the moat there is an archery ground. In the whole fortress site there are several large-calibre guns which command the whole of the port area.

It is well worth taking a walk round the flat roof of the citadel (entrance through the Museu Militar; see below). From there there is a complete panorama over the sea, port, city and mountains.

Museu Militar

The Museu Militar (military museum) is located inside the **citadel**. In the courtyard stand examples of artillery from the 19th and early 20th c. The exhibition is housed in the rooms surrounding the courtyard and in the casemates.

Castell de Montjuïc

© Baedeker

1 Bridge
2 Sant Carles Bastion
3 Santa Amalia Bastion
4 Plaça de Armes
5 Museum entrance
6 Library
7 Picture gallery
8 Toilets
9 Weapons of the Spanish
   Army
10 Spanish armed forces 1981
11 Santa Elena Moat

12 Velasco Bulwark
13 Water reservoir
14 Transformer station
15 Lengua Serpe Bastion
16 Secret door
17 Outwork facing the sea
18 Outwork facing the land
19 Moat
20 Archery ground
21 Secret door
22 Battlement walk
23 Battlement walk

From the gateway, where the ticket office is located, the visitor turns left and views the exhibition in a clockwise direction. The **library** (Rooms 3 and 4) can be visited by prior arrangement. From there we go downstairs into the **casemates** (Rooms 1–7; photography is forbidden here). In the smaller room on the left and in the neighbouring rooms can be seen displays of blank weapons, firearms, models of battleships and fighting planes, a large model of Montjuïc, as well as models of other Spanish castles, landscape dioramas of historic battlegrounds. On the wall there is a large map showing the individual *comarques* (districts) and important castles of Catalonia, and a collection of tin soldiers. In the large room (at the bottom of the stairs on the right) there are medieval and more recent weapons (crossbows, flails, armour and firearms).

The tour then returns to the **courtyard**; here are the auditorium (Room 6) and newly furnished rooms (Room 7 onwards). These contain more historical weapons, extensive collections of modern firearms (handguns from various sources, automatic weapons) and uniforms of various military units. Non-military material is to be found in Room 18, where items connected with the history of the mountain and finds from the old Jewish cemetery can be seen.

From the inner courtyard visitors can go up to the large roof terrace, from which there are splendid **views**.

Open Tue.–Sat.
9.30am–1.30pm,
3.30–7.30pm,
Sun., pub. hols.
10am–8pm (7pm
Oct.–Mar.)

★Parc d'Atraccions

Montjuïc is famous above all for the Parc d'Atraccions (**amusement park**) on its north-eastern slope. There are large car parks available near the

◀ *Amusement park on Montjuïc*

The inner courtyard of the citadel, Montjuïc

Open Tue.–Sun. in high season; other times Sat., Sun., pub. hols.

entrances. The park is basically a large permanent fairground with 40 rides, including a big wheel, roller coasters and other similar rides (ghost train, bumper cars); plus an open-air theatre, amusement arcades and a restaurant.

Another amusement park is located on Tibidabo (see entry).

Further down from the amusement park we come to the **Mirador del Alcalde** with its fountains and superb view across the inner city area and the harbour. The paving in the pedestrian area is very unusual, consisting of concrete pipes, necks and bases from bottles, and transmission chains, all decoratively arranged.

Jardins de Mossèn Jacint Verdaguer

To the west of the amusement park, stretching downhill to the Plaça Dante and the lower station of the chairlift are the Jardins de Mossèn Jacint Verdaguer, named after the famous Catalan poet (1845–1902). The largest part of the gardens is made up of water terraces on either side of the steps which are covered with water lilies. An inscription stone bears the words of a poem by Verdaguer.

★Jardins de Mossèn Costa i Llobera

The steep slope of Montjuïc which faces the sea is occupied by the extensive Jardins de Mossèn Costa i Llobera (named after the poet Miquel Costa i Llobera who was a contemporary of Verdaguer). They are reached from the Plaça Dante by crossing the Avinguda de Miramar.

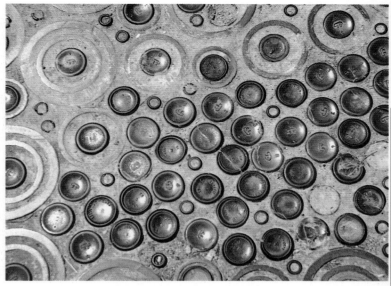

The original decorative pavement of the Mirador del Alcalde

Water terraces in the Jardins de Mossèn Jacint Verdaguer

Cacti in the Jardins de Mossèn Costa i Llobera

Plaça de l'Armada

Near the upper station of the port cable railway lies the Plaça de l'Armada, from where there is a good view of the harbour and the Old Town. In the small adjoining **Jardins de Miramar** is a statue of a woman by Josep Clarà.

Right by the square is the upper entrance to the **Jardins de Mossèn Costa i Llobera**. This park is very well set out and is famous for its large stocks of succulents, cacti and euphorbias. On a platform there is the bronze statue of a lacemaker by the sculptor Josep Viladomat.

The visitor goes back to the Plaça Dante, passing the Fundació Joan Miró (see entry). In the western part of Montjuïc are to be found part of the sports facilities which are being substantially enlarged for the Olympic Games (see Olympic Sites), the Museu Arqueològic (see entry), the Museu Etnològic (see entry), the Palau Nacional (see entry), the Botanical Gardens (see entry), the Poble Espanyol (see entry), and the new **Mercat de les Flors** (a theatre converted from a flower market).

★Montseny

Excursion
50 km (31 mi.) NE

The massif of Montseny lies almost 50 km (31 mi.) to the north-east of Barcelona and 30 km (19 mi.) inland from the Costa Daurada. This mountainous area is where the Riu Tordera has its source.

Serra de Montseny

The Serra de Montseny is a low mountain range almost completely covered by forest. At the Turó del Home it reaches 1712 m (5617 ft) and this represents the highest point in the Catalan coastal range. Important sources of income are forestry and agriculture; tourism also plays a role, for the national park which lies within the area is very popular for walking and recreation.

From Sant Celoni, situated in the valley of the Riu Tordera, a very winding but extremely scenic road with fine views across to Santa Fe del Montseny (altitude 1100 m (3609 ft)), the most important locality within the national park. The village has grown up around a former abbey and today forms a good base for mountain walking. To the west rises the Turó del Home, the summit of which offers superb views in all directions and is the site of a meteorological station.

Santa Fe del
Montseny

★★Montserrat

Montserrat, famed for its monastery, rises some 1220 m (4000 ft) above the plain to the north-west of Barcelona. The visitor wishing to drive from Barcelona to Montserrat is advised to leave the city centre on the Avingunda de la Diagonal in a south-west direction and soon this road merges with the motorway to Martorell. From Martorell follow the main road which goes via Olesa to Monistrol. A short way beyond Olesa a bridge across the valley leads to the cableway (large sign "Aerí"; officially Funicular Aerí del Montserrat) the upper station of which is situated right by the monastery on the mountain. There is also a direct rail line from Barcelona to the cableway, leaving from the station beneath the Plaça d'Espanya. (A combined train, cable car and funicular ticket is available, and there are organised half-day coach tours.)

Excursion
50 km (31 mi.) NW

Access The road up to Montserrat (8 km (5 mi.), at times very steep but well engineered) branches off the main road in Monistrol and winds up the mountain offering fine views of the surrounding country. The road ends at the monastery where there is a large car park.

History Montserrat was at one time erroneously thought to be the Monsalvatsch in Wolfram von Eschenbach's saga of the Holy Grail. It is now considered much more likely that the latter is to be found at Salvatierra, a place of pilgrimage on the southern side of the Pyrenees. According to legend the monastery was founded in the year 880 in honour of a miracle-working statue of the Virgin Mary; the first documentary mention dates from 888. In 976 it was handed over to the Benedictine order and in 1025 was considerably enlarged by monks from the Catalan towns of Ripoll and Vich. In 1409 Pope Benedict XIII raised it to the status of an independent abbey and towards the end of the century the monastic printing house was installed. A former monk of Montserrat travelled with Columbus's fleet to the New World in 1493 and he is reputed to have named the island of Montserrat, which forms part of the Lesser Antilles (and is today a British Crown Colony). In 1522 Ignatius Loyola, who later was to found the Jesuit order, spent some time in the monastery. At the beginning of the 19th c. Napoleon's troops forced their way into Spain; the enormous riches of the monastery became lost during the War of Liberation (from 1808 onwards) and the convent was destroyed in 1811 by the French. More severe losses were brought about by the closure of the monastery during the Carlist Wars (1835–60). The monastery still has its associated school of sacred music ("Escolania"), founded in the 15th c. It is the custom for its youthful members to sing the Salve at the time of Ave Maria (1pm) and also at vespers. The main festivals of Montserrat are on April 27th and September 8th.

Montsagrat

Montserrat ("sawn mountain"), the Montsagrat (sacred mountain) of the Catalans, is one of the greatest attractions for visitors in the whole of

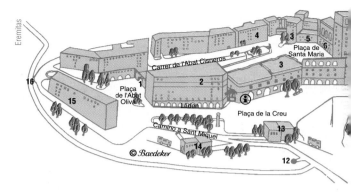

Erenitas

Carrer de l'Abat Cisneros

Plaça de Santa Maria

Plaça de l'Abat Oliva

Laden

Plaça de la Creu

Camino a Sant Miquel

© *Baedeker*

1 Main entrance to Monastery
  area
2 Audiovisual Information
3 Museum in two buildings
4 Hotel

5 Gothic cloister
6 Gateway Building
7 Basilica
8 Song School
  (Escolania)

Spain, both for its scenery and for its famous monastery. It is a massive conglomerate 10 km (6 mi.) long and 5 km (3 mi.) wide, which towers up out of the Catalan plateau, in an almost isolated position across the right bank of the Riu Llobregat and sloping steeply downwards on all sides. With its fantastic rock images formed by erosion it looks from a distance like a huge castle. The highest point in the massif is the 1241-m (4073-ft) mountain Sant Jeroni. From the south-east the mountain is bisected by a huge cleft in the rocks known as the "Vall Malalt" (evil valley). The monastery stands at its beginning on an outcrop at an altitude of 725 m (2379 ft). The north-east slope is covered by pine woods, the other sides and the summit by evergreen bushes. The famous flora of the mountain (there are some 1500 plant varieties) was largely destroyed in 1986 by fires.

★Montserrat Monastery

Open daily
6am–8pm

The monastery with its basilica and neighbouring buildings virtually forms a small self-contained town in itself. The road ends at the large car park. Here the visitor has access to an extensive observation terrace on which stands a modern monument to the Catalan poet and mystic, Ramón Llull (or Raymond Lully; c. 1235–1316), who was born in Palma de Mallorca. The eight steps of the monument resemble a spiral staircase and are called the "steps of knowledge" (stone, fire, plants, animals, human beings, angels, God). Close by stands a circular memorial to the dead.

The inner part of the monastery complex is reached by crossing the Plaça de la Creu ("square of the cross", named after the sculpture of a cross dating from 1927 on the left-hand side). Around the square are souvenir shops, a restaurant, post office, telephone kiosks and an exchange office. Audio-visual information about Montserrat is available every 30 minutes at the bottom of the steps. On the Plaça de l'Abat Oliba, near the main entrance to the monastery, farmers wives from the outlying villages sell their produce.

From here the visitor enters a broad square, the Plaça de Santa Maria. To the right of the wide central avenue leading to the basilica is the

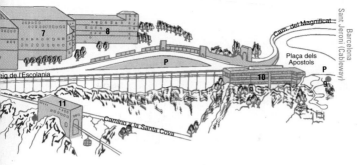

Montserrat

9 Monument to Ramon Llul
10 Restaurant
11 Cableway Lower Station
   (Funicular Aerí)
12 Monument to Pau (Pablo) Casals

13 Funicular to the Sacred Grotto
   (Cova Santa)
14 Funicular to Sant Joan
15 Gendarmerie (Guarda Civil)
16 Via Crucis (Way of the Cross)

entrance to the new section of the **Museu de Montserrat**, which is situated beneath the square. (A ticket is valid for both sections of the museum.) This section contains works by Catalan painters of the 19th and 20th c. and is mainly of regional interest.

*Open daily
10.30am–2pm,
3–6pm*

The old section is to be found diagonally left of the main façade of the church and contains a small Egyptian collection (several copies of well-known large sculptures, small terracottas, seals, a human mummy and two sarcophagi). There are also finds from the neolithic period, Roman and Byzantine ceramics and ornaments, coins, antique glass, and Jewish objects of worship (tallit – prayer coat, schofare – ram's horns for ritual use, Torah scrolls).

Further to the left, below the rock, is the Hostal Abad Cisneros (hotel).

At the end of the square stands a **gatehouse**, with five arches in its lower part, three in the upper. It was built between 1942 and 1968 and marks the boundary of the actual area of the church. The reliefs in the three upper arches show (from the left) St Benedict, the Assumption of Mary (according to the dogma of Pope Pius XII) and St George, the patron saint of Catalonia. From time to time groups of pilgrims from Catalonia gather to dance the sardana, a national folk dance. To the left of the façade can be seen the remains of the former Gothic **cloister** (15th c.).

Between the gatehouse and the actual church there is a fairly narrow inner courtyard with a statue of St Benedict (1927) and next to it the gateway to the monastery (not open to the public). The decorative graffiti on the side façades are modern. The baptistry, which is situated inside the gatehouse building, also opens out onto the inner courtyard. Its entrance is surrounded by decorative 20th c. reliefs.

The **basilica**, which contains the highly revered statue of the Madonna, dates from the 18th c. but was substantially altered and rebuilt during the 19th and 20th c. The façade shows Renaissance forms, although the figures of Christ and the apostles were only added in 1900.

Interior There are two entrances into the church: the main entrance leads into the nave, while the right-hand side door gives direct access to the Madonna (one way only).

The nave inside is 68 m (223 ft) long, 21 m (69 ft) wide and 33 m (108 ft) high; it is dimly lit by large numbers of votive candles. The interior decoration is modern (19th–20th c.).

The **Madonna of Montserrat**, the "Santa Imatge" of the Catalans, is one of the most important objects of pilgrimage in the whole of Spain. As is frequently the case in Spanish churches, it stands high up behind the high altar and is reached by steps leading from the transept. The staircases are framed by beaten silver ornamentation. The coloured wooden sculpture dates from the 12th or 13th c; the face and hands have become darkened with age and for this reason is called **"la Moreneta"** (the brown lady). Legend has it that the sculpture is the work of St Luke, who was brought to Spain by St Peter. The chapel containing "la Moreneta" may be visited daily 8–10.30am, noon–1.30pm, and 3–6.30pm.

The visitor leaves the church by the left transept. Outside on the wall of the rock there are many votive gifts (including wax limbs as thanks for healing) and offertory candles as well as the sacred spring ("Mística Font de l'Aigua de la Vida") and near it a coloured majolica madonna.

The Plaça del Abat Oliva is the beginning of the **Via Crucis** (Way of the Cross). The fourteen large groups of statues date from between 1904 and 1919 and were restored after the Civil War. At the end of the Stations of the Cross is a chapel (Verge de la Solitud); from the fourteenth station a path leads to the Ermita Sant Miquel (19th c.), the original building of which existed in the 10th c.

From the Plaça de la Creu there is a path passing the upper station of the cableway (see p. 81) which leads to the **Cova Santa** with its 17th c. chapel. It is said that the Madonna of Montserrat was kept hidden here during the period of the Moorish occupation and was rediscovered by shepherds.

At the Plaça de la Creu is the valley station of the cableway leading to **Sant Joan**. Nearby on the path stands a monument to the Catalan cellist Pau Casals (1876–1973). Sant Joan is one of the thirteen hermitages that once existed in the area of Montserrat; from the upper station there is a beautiful view of the monastery.

A cableway 680 m (2231 ft) long with a 535 m (1755 ft) height difference (the oldest one in Spain) leads from the Manresa road up to the ★★**Capilla de Sant Jeroni**, from where it is a short walk to the summit of Sant Jeroni, which at 1241 m (4073 ft) is the highest point in the massif.

Museu Arqueològic de Barcelona   I 6

Close to the south-eastern edge of the Exhibition Grounds (see entry) and at the foot of Montjuïc (see entry) is the Museu Arqueològic de Barcelona (**Archaeological Museum**). This pseudo-classical circular brick building was originally built as the "Palau d'Arts Gràfiques" for the World Exhibition of 1929, and in 1932 it was enlarged and converted to its present use. The museum's exhibits have their origin in a collection dating back to 1888, which after 1932 was able to be considerably increased through the acquisition of numerous additional items. Today the museum belongs to the Institut de Prehistòria i Arqueologia de la Diputació de Barcelona.

Location
Passeig Santa Madrona

Metro
Poble Sec (L3)

Open Tue.–Sat.
9.30am–1.30pm,
3.30–7pm, Sun.,
pub. hols.
10am–2.30pm

◀ *The monastery on the legendary mountain of Montserrat*

The **tour** of the museum is arranged chronologically and begins with the early development of man (flint tools, a large diorama with the reproduction of an inhabited Stone Age cave). Exhibits from the neolithic include ceramics with ribbon and cord decorations. Megalithic culture is represented by carved models from stone graves. Reproductions of graves from the Bronze Age (El Argar culture) follow on, together with urnfield culture and early metal weapons.

The next section is devoted to the Balearics (Balearic cave culture, Talayot culture). Of particular interest is the gallery focusing on Carthaginian culture in Ibiza, with finds (small terracottas, busts, jewellery) from the famous necropolis on Ibiza town's Puig des Molins. A large model depicts the Greek city of Empùries (Ampurias on the Costa Brava in what today is Girona province) and there is a rich collection of finds from the Magna Graecia (Attic and Etruscan vessels), Terra Sigillata and small bronzes. The newly laid out large hall situated beyond the main entrance and rotunda contains items from the Roman period (amphorae, terracottas, sarcophagae, weapons, a model of the Circus Maximus in Rome). The rotunda itself, two-and-a-half-storeys high, has also been reorganised. The outer display on the ground floor features artefacts from the Iberian culture (ceramic pots, farm implements, small bronzes, weapons and moulds), while the inner display comprises a collection of stone relics including Roman sarcophagae and reliefs. This collection is continued on the first floor of the rotunda where smaller pieces are exhibited. The tour of the museum ends with the Early Christian period and Visigoth culture.

Teatre Grec

Directly beyond the road leading up to Montjuïc is the Teatre Grec (Greek Theatre) situated in an abandoned quarry on the slope of the mountain. It was designed for the 1929 World Exhibition, using Epidauros as a model – albeit on a much smaller scale. Concentric rows of seats surround the deep stage, which even today is used for performances (Greek classics).

The theatre is surrounded by the Baroque-influenced Jardí Amargs.

Espai Escénic Municipal

To the west opposite the museum stands the building of the former **Mercat dels Flors** (Flower Market) now the Espai Escénic Municipal (municipal theatre centre) offering an extremely varied programme of events.

Museu Clarà   D 7

Location
Carrer Calatrava
27–29

Railway station
(FGC)
Tres Torres

Open Tue.–Sun.
9.30am–1.30pm

The Museu Clarà is situated in the select residential area of Sant Gervasi. The sculptor Josep Clarà (1889–1958) occupied the small property until his death; in 1969 the museum, which contains the most important examples of his work, was opened.

The exhibits most worth seeing are the sculptures (statues), and also the paintings and graphics. A small section is devoted to souvenirs from his personal belongings and works by artists who had close ties of friendship with him. In the small garden are two marble blocks which form part of the artist's legacy and on which lines by the poet Joan Maragall have been engraved.

Museu d'Art Contemporani   H 9

Location
Plaça dels Angels

Metro
Universitat (L1,
L2), Catalunya
(L1, L3)

South-west of the Ramblas, in the heart of the very dilapidated Barri Xino (see entry), stands the Casa de Caritat (see entry), to which has recently been added the modern, dazzling white building of the Museu d'Art Contemporani (MACBA; **Museum of Contemporary Art**). There could hardly be a greater contrast.

That the Museu d'Art Modern in the Parc de la Ciutadella lacked space for the ever-growing collection of contemporary art became apparent a

The glass façade of the Museum of Contemporary Art

long time ago; hence the inauguration in late 1995 of this new building, designed by the US architect Richard Meier. The permanent collection is still being assembled, so temporary exhibitions are currently being shown.

The huge main façade with its vast expanse of glass overlooks the Plaça dels Angels (not to be confused with the Plaça del Angel near to the Museu d'Història de la Ciutat), so called after a convent of that name which once stood here.

Museu d'Art de Catalunya

See Palau Nacional

Museu d'Art Modern   I 12

The **Museum of Modern Art** (MNAC) has since 1945 been housed in the left wing of the Palau de la Ciutadella where the Parliament of Catalonia (regional parliament) is also situated. The Municipal Palace was built in the 18th c. as an arsenal, the museum wing being added at the start of the 20th c.

The term "Museum of Modern Art" is somewhat misleading, for the exhibits – predominantly works by Catalan artists – go back in time via Historicism to the Romantic period. Correspondingly, in the older sections, most of which are arranged in chronological order, the themes are conventional (portraits, genre scenes, landscapes, a few large historical paintings). Of interest is the Art Nouveau section (furniture, pictures, sculpture), and also Expressionist and early modern works and sculptures from the early 20th c.

Location
Parc de la
Ciutadella

Metro
Ciutadella (L4)

Open Tue.–Sat.
10am–7pm,
Sun., pub. hols.
10am–2.30pm

87

The Passeig
de Colom,
extending
north from the
Columbus
Monument

The visitor then goes up a staircase to the upper floor where special temporary exhibitions are held.

In all the museum provides a representative but fairly restrictive survey of Spanish art (especially Catalan) since about 1830 but is of interest more from the standpoint of art history and less in a general sense.

The Contemporary Art section, which still occupies a comparatively small area, is being transferred in stages to the new Museu d'Art Contemporani (see entry).

Museu d'Art Precolombí   I 10

Location
Carrer Montcada
14

Metro
Barceloneta (L 4)

Recently the Museu d'Art Precolombí (**Museum of Pre-Columbian Art**) has been housed in the same building as the Museu Textil (see entry). It contains some of the Swiss Barbier-Mueller collection and currently includes some two hundred exhibits from Central and South America (culture of the Maya, Aztecs, Olmecs, Incas). The exhibition is scheduled to end in the year 2001, and may then be acquired by Catalonia.

Museu d'Autómates

See Tibidabo

★Museu de Cera   I 9

Location
Passatge de la
Banca 7

Metro
Drassanes (L3)

Open Mon.–Fri.
10am–1.30pm,
4–7.30pm, Sat.,
Sun., pub. hols.
10am–1.30pm,
4.30–8pm

The Museu de Cera (**Waxworks**) is located at the port end of the Ramblas (see entry) in a rather old-fashioned 19th c. building. The founder of the museum, Enrique Alarcón, a great cineast, has created an eerily beautiful display by means of regularly changing groups of more than 300 wax figures in all, although the characters represented are identifiable less by their physiognomic similarity than by their clothing and the general atmosphere.

The visitor reaches the museum through a small inner courtyard and then turns right (where the ticket office is situated) into an annexe which houses the "Expo-Museum", containing exclusively figures from Hollywood film history.

The main part of the museum is in the building with the high façade which encloses the inner courtyard. This building, largely unrestored and decorated inside with wall and ceiling paintings, gives a good impression of the architecture of the early Modernist period. The tour of the museum begins on the **first floor** where a double representation of Pope John Paul II greets the visitor. This is followed by large groups of artistic and political figures of past times (including Pau Casals, Andrés Segovia, the Shah of Persia, George Sand and Frédéric Chopin), fairy-tale characters, and dictators such as Francisco Franco, Adolf Hitler, Mussolini and Mao Tse-Tung. The world of opera is represented by Richard Wagner, Ludwig von Beethoven, Plácido Domingo, Maria Callas and others (with an appropriate soundtrack). Then follow artists (Francisco Goya and Maja, Pablo Picasso, Joan Miró, Diego Velázquez, Salvador Dalí) and writers (William Shakespeare, Miguel de Cervantes, Pedro Calderón, Jean-Baptiste Molière, and behind them Don Quixote, Sancho Panza and Dulcinea).

Scientists and artists from the turn of the 19th c. are gathered together in a coffee-house atmosphere.

On the **second floor** there is a group of film stars, assembled on the swaying deck of an ocean liner, rulers and knights from the late

Middle Ages and the Renaissance period, as well as famous sports personalities.

A lift brings the visitor down to the **ground floor** and the "Viaje Ficción" section ("Fantastic journey"). By means of a deep-sea diving bell and an underwater tunnel the visitor reaches a fantasy world (between the decks on a sailing ship, dripstone cave with Stone Age men, space journey and science fiction monster). On the far side of the souvenir kiosk is the "Terror" section (Alfred Hitchcock; various forms of execution; Bonnie and Clyde in the bank safe). The final exhibit is the "Horror" cabinet with Frankenstein, Dracula and Dr Mabuse.

Museu de Ceràmica

See Palau de Pedralbes

Museu de Geologia   I 11

The museums in the Parc de la Ciutadella (see entry) include the Museu de Geologia (**Geological Museum**; also known as the Museu Martorell, after its founder). It is linked with the Institute of Natural Sciences. Opened in 1882, it is housed in a low Neo-Classical building which was built for the 1888 World Exhibition, and is the first museum building in Barcelona designed to be used as such from the outset.

The entrance is in the gabled central section of the side facing the park. In the rooms to the left of the entrance hall can be seen minerals, mainly precious and semi-precious stones (including copies in rock-crystal of the largest known diamonds) as well as exhibits showing the technical applications of precious and non-ferrous metals. The minerals are arranged according to their chemical structure.

At the end of the hall, distinguishable by the light shining through the agate panes, is a darkened room with minerals bathed in long and short-wave ultraviolet light, producing interesting luminous effects.

The room to the right of the hallway contains mainly fossils.

Location
Parc de la
Ciutadella

Metro
Arc de Triomf (L1)
Ciutadella (L4)

Open Tue.–Sun.
10am–2pm

Next to the Geological Museum stands the Palm House with its exotic flora.   **Palm House**

Museu de la Catedral

See Cathedral

Museu de la Ciència   C 9

The Museu del Ciència (**Science Museum**) lies at the foot of Tibidabo (see entry). It is sponsored by the Caixa de Pensions de Catalunya (Pension Insurance Company of Catalonia), which is also active in other spheres as a supporter of cultural pursuits. The museum building, erected for charitable purposes in the early 20th c., has been suitably extended. Nearby runs the city ring road, constructed specially for the Olympic Games and separating the museum from Tibidabo.

The aim of the extensive experimental collection is to explain – mainly by means of simple experiments which people can carry out themselves – natural history phenomena and relationships to as wide a spectrum of the populace as possible. The main emphasis is on ecology, optical, accoustic and sensorial awareness, with considerable space devoted to each.

Location
Carrer Roviralta
66

Railway station
(FGC)
Avinguda del
Tibidabo

Open Tue.–Sun.
10am–8pm

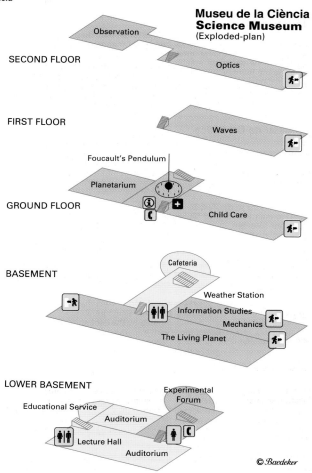

Museu de la Ciència
Science Museum
(Exploded-plan)

SECOND FLOOR — Observation, Optics

FIRST FLOOR — Waves

GROUND FLOOR — Foucault's Pendulum, Planetarium, Child Care

BASEMENT — Cafeteria, Weather Station, Information Studies, Mechanics, The Living Planet

LOWER BASEMENT — Experimental Forum, Educational Service, Auditorium, Lecture Hall, Auditorium

© Baedeker

On the central reservation of the ring road outside the museum, an old submarine has been put on display, partly opened up to expose the interior.

The museum is particularly valuable for children of primary-school age upwards, not least because of the many opportunities for personal experiments and activities; they should spend at least half a day there.

For smaller children there is a playroom (with child minders), equipped with toys on specific themes.

Planetarium   The museum also has a separate Planetarium with a demonstration lasting about 30 minutes (additional charge).

There is another Planetarium (see entry) on the Carrer de les Ecole Pies.

Museu de la Música   F 10

In the Avenida de la Diagonal, which cuts across the Eixample district of the city, near the Plaça de Joan Carles I which forms the junction with the Passeig de Gràcia, lies the Museu de la Música (**Music Museum**), founded in 1947. The house in which it is contained was built in 1902 by the architect Josep Puig i Cadafalch. It is one of the most important examples of Modernisme (see Baedeker Special p. 30) and worth seeing just on that account. The museum exhibits are systematically arranged according to the physics of sound production.

Location
Diagonal 373

Metro
Diagonal (L3, L5)

Open Tue.–Sun.
10am–2pm,
Wed 5–8pm

A very attractive little courtyard leads via steps to the first of the former living areas; from here a lift goes up to the fourth floor where there are rooms for educational use and for mounting small temporary exhibitions. The **signposted tour** starts on the third floor with the string instruments. The collection of guitars, some from as far back as the 17th c., is one of the most comprehensive in Europe. The collection of instruments played with a bow is likewise noteworthy. There are also psalters, harps, lutes, balalaikas and mandolins, many of them richly decorated with intarsia work. Unusual individual items include a violin made from blue painted porcelain and another in the shape of a walking stick.

Brass and woodwind instruments are displayed down the stairs on the second floor, keyboard instruments – mainly harpsichords and organs – on the first floor (where note the lavish decor of what were once living rooms).

The museum also contains a collection of music reproduction equipment, a record library and a specialist library. The staff are happy to give advice on technical matters.

Museu de la Sagrada Família

See Sagrada Família

Museu del Calçat   I 9

On the little Plaça de Felip Neri, to the south-west near the cathedral (for location see Barri Gòtic, detailed plan), stands a pretty Renaissance building that was once the headquarters of the municipal shoemakers' guild.

It now houses the Museu del Calçat (**Shoe Museum**) that traces the historical development of shoes and shoemaking, a craft rich in traditions. The large collection focuses mainly on Catalonia.

Location
Plaça Felip Neri

Metro
Liceu (L3)

Open Tue.–Sun.
11am–2pm

The Plaça Felip Neri was named after the Italian Filippo Neri (1515–95) who was canonised in 1622 and who founded the Order of Oratorians in 1575. The Barcelona congregation (commonly known as "Felipons") was founded towards the end of the 17th c.; the **Oratorian College** was built in 1673 and remodelled in the 18th c. Typical of the Counter-Reformation, it shows Baroque influence, something of a rarity in Barcelona. The exterior walls have bullet holes sustained in the Civil War, when a number of Oratorian monks were shot.

Museu del Futbol Club Barcelona   E 3

A little way to the south-east, adjoining the Zona Universitaria, on land designed to provide Olympic facilities (see Olympic Sites), lies the huge stadium (Camp Nou) of the famous F.C. Barcelona football club, with some 125,000 seats, making it one of the largest in the world.

Location
Carrer Arístides
Maillol

Metro
Collblanc (L5)

The club, several times national champions and European Cup winners, has its own **museum** here (via Gate 2 of the entrance pavilion), displaying trophies and historical documents as well as an audiovisual show on several screens.

A good general view of the stadium can be had from the president's box. Open Mon.–Sat. 10am–6.30pm, Sun., pub. hols. 10am–2pm. Closed Jan. 6th, Sep. 24th, Dec. 25th

Museu del Llibre i de les Arts Gràfiques

See Poble Espanyol

Museu del Perfum   G 10

Location
Passeig de Gràcia
39

Metro
Passeig de Gràcia
(L2, L3, L4)

A private perfume company has its offices on the broad Passeig de Gràcia (see entry), and runs a small specialised museum. This provides an interesting insight into the history of fragrances and scents, including highly artistic antique containers, bottles and the like, from the Baroque period (17th–18th c.) to the present day. Open Mon.–Fri. 10am–1.30pm, 4–7pm. Closed pub. hols.

Museu del Temple Expiatori de la Sagrada Família

See Sagrada Família

Museu de Zoologia   I 11

Location
Parc de la
Ciutadella

Metro
Arc de Triomf (L1)
Ciutadella (L4)

Open Tue.–Sun.
10am–2pm

The Museu de Zoologia (**Zoological Museum**) stands at the western end of the Parc de la Ciutadella (see entry). This somewhat unique building in a pseudo-Moorish mixture of styles was erected by Lluís Domènech i Montaner as a gastronomic concern for the 1888 World Exhibition, and is popularly known as the "castell dels tres dragons" ("Three Dragons Castle").

Temporary exhibitions are held on the **ground floor**, where there is also a comprehensive insect collection and skeletons of a whale and a mammoth. Other glass cabinets contain mussels and snails as well as stuffed birds.

A staircase with an attractive stairwell leads to the **upper floor**, which houses the major part of the permanent exhibitions. These include a collection of birds' eggs, stuffed mammals (with corresponding skeletons by the side), and preserved molluscs, fish, reptiles and amphibians. At the end of the large main hall, behind a glass door, can be seen a conchological study collection (mussel and snail shells).

All the collections are used for research and teaching purposes. Although its layout is extremely antiquated the museum is spotlessly clean and orderly and possesses considerable nostalgic charm. It is currently being extended.

★★Museu d'Història de la Ciutat   I 10

Location
Plaça del Rei

Metro
Jaume I (L4)

On the Plaça del Rei stands the Casa Clariana Padellás (originally built near by in the 15th c. and rebuilt on its present site in 1931), a typical medieval urban palace. Important remains of the old Roman town were discovered when excavating for the foundations on its new site, which led the authorities to decide to make the building a Historical Museum.

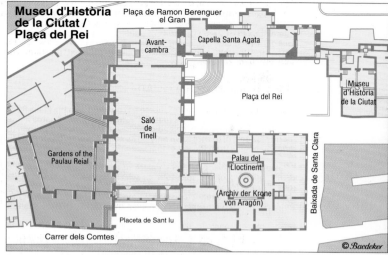

Museu d'Història de la Ciutat / Plaça del Rei

Plaça de Ramon Berenguer el Gran

Capella Santa Agata

Avant-cambra

Plaça del Rei

Museu d'Història de la Ciutat

Saló de Tinell

Gardens of the Paulau Reial

Palau del Lloctinent

(Archiv der Krone von Aragón)

Baixada de Santa Clara

Placeta de Sant Iu

Carrer dels Comtes

© *Baedeker*

The secular church on higher ground and a large room in the former royal palace (see Museu Frederic Marés), the **Saló de Tinell** built in 1370, also belong to the museum. The latter is where Christopher Columbus was received by the Catholic Monarchs on his return from his first voyage to America.

Open Tue.–Sat. 10am–2pm, 4–8pm (Jun.–Sep. 10am–8pm), Sun., pub. hols. 10am–2pm

In the basement can be seen the uncovered remains of the **Roman town** (with excellent printed information provided), as well as models of the excavations in display cabinets. The remains include parts of the heating system, mosaic floors, parts of the surrounding walls and the water and drainage systems. Also of interest is the large oil mill with big bulbous receptacles in situ. From the cellars visitors can enter a narrow shaft set vertically in the town wall, where they can see how the old Roman hidden passages and the like were blocked up during the Middle Ages.

Then proceed further up the stairs to rooms 12–16. In the stairwell can be seen a collection of copper pots and pans as well as colourful glazed tiles (everyday scenes, animals and human beings; see also Museu de Ceramica).

In Room 12 a form of family tree shows the various trade guilds with the names of their patrons.

In Room 13 will be found a number of historical panels. In Room 14 are wooden stamps used for textile printing as well as examples of materials; on the wall hangs a painting, dating from the first half of the 19th c., of a clothing shop in Barcelona.

Room 11 contains a quantity of sketches illustrating the historical development of the city; of particular interest is the large plan for the redevelopment of the Eixample (see entry), by Ildefons Cerdà, signed June 7th 1859, with the original lithograph stones. In Room 10 hang a number of historical paintings.

The stairs then lead up to the second floor which is at present closed; however, the terrace, from which there is an excellent view of the Plaça del Rei, is worth seeing.

The Galeria de Catalans il·lustres (see entry) in the Carrer del Bisbe Caçador also belongs to the museum.

The **Barcelona Punt Zero** is a series of guided tours through the historical quarter of the city, beginning at 10am. Detailed information can be obtained and the obligatory advance booking made at the Museum Information Service (Carrer de Verguer 2; tel. 933151111).

Plaça del Rei

The Plaça del Rei ("King's Square"; not to be confused with the Plaça Reial near the Ramblas – see entry), is one of the most beautiful squares in the old town. It is surrounded by splendid medieval buildings and is open to the narrow streets of the old town only on its southern side. The following description begins from the left of that opening and proceeds clockwise.

The **Palau del Lloctinent del Rei** ("Palace of the Royal Lieutenant") is a cold, flat building of the mid-16th c., which houses the Arxiu de la Corona d'Aragó (Archives of the Crown of Aragón). The coats of arms of the heads of state are repeated several times on the façade. The colourful inner courtyard represents the transition from Gothic to Renaissance.

Opposite the entrance to the Plaça stands the square Romanesque building, the **Saló del Tinell** (Throne Room), dominated by a rectangular tower in the Tuscan style. The giant hall, spanned by broad, semicircular arched girders, is of historical importance: it was here that Christopher Columbus, following his first expedition to the New World, was received almost as an equal by the Spanish rulers Ferdinand II and Isabella I (the "Reyes Católicos"). The hall is entered through an anteroom, which is connected with the square by a semicircular open staircase. Temporary exhibitions are held here from time to time.

The **Capella Santa Agata**, built in the Gothic style on the old Roman town wall, and now a secular building, was once the royal palace chapel. It is also accessible via the above-mentioned open staircase.
   The single-naved interior contains a Gothic picture-altar, two Gothic gravestones high up and some priests' cells; the former sacristy has a large iron mechanical clock dating from the year 1576.
   The old windows in the choir and gallery show the various coats-of-arms of the counts of Barcelona.

Museu Frederic   See entry
Marès

Plaça de l'Angel

The Plaça de l'Angel is at the junction of Via Laietana and Carrer Jaume I, which leads from the Plaça de Sant Jaume and continues into Carrer de la Princesa. To the right, just off the wide main street leading to the south-east, can be seen remains of the old town wall, on which stands the Palau de Requesens (see Galeria de Catalans il·lustres).

Museu d'Història de la Medicina de Catalunya   G 9

Location
Passatge Mercader
11

Metro
Diagonal (L3, L5)

The Museu d'Història de la Medicina de Catalunya (**Museum of Medicine**) houses in fourteen rooms some 2,500 exhibits illustrative of the principal developments in medical practice, especially in anatomy, epidemiology, physiology and bacteriology. Special exhibitions can be seen in the basement.

The foundation which supports the museum also conducts specialist events for medical students.

Currently closed for refurbishment.

Museu d'Holografia   I 10

The Museu d'Holografia (**Holographic Museum**) is the first of its kind in Spain. This little museum, resembling a gallery, is reached from the Plaça Sant Jaume through the Carrer Jaume I, where the entrance to the first building opens off on the left.

Holography is a new achievement in three-dimensional pattern-producing techniques which only became fully practicable following the development of lasers. Objects wrapped in plastic sheets and subjected to interference between a coherent light beam and light defracted from the same beam by the object produce a solid-looking picture (also in colour). According to the position of the observer and the angle at which the light falls, the foreground and background appear to move closer or further away, various degrees of movement being detectable.

The impression produced by the hologram set up on the first floor (be careful of the cross-beam in the stairwell) is truly breathtaking: it may be a confusion of spiral springs and wood shavings shooting out of the frame, a large flower springing towards the observer or the portrait of a Rocker who suddenly spits large splinters of glass out of his mouth – the illusion (without the need for special spectacles or anything like that) is complete.

On the ground floor there is a large selection of holograms for sale, ranging from cheap plaques to larger items costing thousands of pesetas or more (up to 40 × 50 cm (16 × 20 in.) in size).

Location
Carrer Jaume I 1

Metro
Jaume I (L4)

Open Mon.–Sat.
10.30am–1.30pm,
5.30–8.30pm

Museu Diocesà   I 10

The Museu Diocesà de Barcelona (**Barcelona Diocesan Museum**) is situated on the narrow Carrer Bisbe, in the immediate vicinity of the cathedral. It houses some of the diocesan archives and has a collection of religious art, mainly from the diocesan area, including some remarkable Romanesque works. Also of interest are the collection's sculptures, paintings, ceramic and goldsmith's work as well as liturgical vestments dating from the early middle ages almost to the present day.

Location
Carrer Bisbe 5

Metro
Jaume I (L4)

Open Tue.–Sat.
10am–2pm,
5pm–8pm,
Sun. 11am–2pm

Museu Egipci

The Museu Egipci was established in 1994 at the same time as the Clos Archaeological Foundation. With some 300 exhibits distributed over three rooms, the collection is not particularly large; but what it lacks in size, it makes up for in quality. There are finds from each period of advanced Egyptian civilisation.

The finest pieces, among them a bust of the lion-headed goddess Sachmet, are displayed on the entrance level. The basement is mainly given over to small items (grave goods, amulets, statuettes and small bronzes) from Ptolemaic and Roman times. On the upper floor there are mummified animals (cat, crocodile, ibis) and a copy of the famous tri-lingual Rosetta Stone that provided the key for deciphering hieroglyphs.

Location
Rambla de
Catalunya 57

Metro
Passeig de Gràcia
(L2, L3, L4)

Open Mon.–Sun.
10am–2pm,
4–8pm

Museu Etnogràfic Andino-Amazonia   D 5

The Museu Etnogràfic Andino-Amazonia (also known as the Museu Etnografico-Missional, **Ethnographic Museum of the Andean and Amazonian Regions**) is in the care of the Capuchin order of monks in

Location
Carrer Cardenal
Vives i Tutó 2–16

Museu Etnològic

Metro
Maria Christina
(L3)

Open by
appointment;
tel. 932043458

Catalonia and is housed in their monastery buildings. The small but extremely well cared for and displayed collection is specialised and covers the native cultures in those areas of Latin America where the order has missions.

A monk (he should be addressed as "padre") will guide you through the museum; a knowledge of Spanish will be a great help in understanding him. On display are small works of art, prepared slides and skeletons of Central American animals, a collection of butterflies and insects and also weapons. On leaving the museum it is customary to make a suitable donation "para el monasterio", i.e. "for the monastery".

Museu Etnològic   I 5

Location
Passeig de Santa
Madrona

Autobus
61 (Placa
Espanya)

Open daily
10am–2pm; Sep.
24th–Jun. 24th
Tue., Thu.
10am–7pm

The Museu Etnològic (**Ethnological Museum**) is situated on a bend in the Passeig de Santa Madrona, which leads up from the Exhibition Centre to Montjuïc (see entries). Built in 1973 and specially designed for exhibitions, the building consists of ajacent hexagons, with generous areas of glass providing ideal space for displays.

The emphasis of the collections (which currently comprise over 20,000 items) is on the cultures of Asia, Africa, America and Oceania, covering biological, ethnographic, cultural and social aspects.

The huge stock of exhibits which the museum possesses means that only temporary specialised displays on individual themes can be on display at any one time, so before arranging a visit it is advisable to obtain details of the current subjects covered (tel. 934246402). The museum also provides an educational service and a specialist library. Open Tue.–Sat. 9am–2pm.

There is also a branch of the museum (Museu d'Arts, Indústries i Tradicions Populars) in Poble Espanyol (see entry).

★Museu Frederic Marès   I 10

Location Caffer
Comtes de
Barcelona 10

Metro
Jaume I (L4)

Open Tue.–Sat.
10am–5pm,
Sun., pub. hols.
10am–2pm

On display in the museum is the former private collection of the sculptor Frederic Marès Deulovol which was donated to the city; in addition to religious art there is a large department devoted to cultural history from the 15th to early 20th c. from the private library of Marès. The beautiful building in which it has been housed since 1946 forms part of the Salò de Tinell complex (see Museu d'Història de la Ciutat).

Access to the museum is through an archway from the Carrer dels Comtes de Barcelona, leading into a picturesque inner courtyard. The **ground floor** contains an outstanding collection of Romanesque and Gothic sacred works of art (particularly crucifixes, the Romanesque being most impressive, and a number of pictures believed to have miraculous powers). Adjoining this is a collection of large and small Roman sculptures.

In the "**crypt**" is an extensive lapidarium (stone engravings from the Early Christian, Romanesque and Gothic periods); the foundations contain a small part of the Roman town wall. Note the two Romanesque portals with rounded arches, one still with the original wood-panelled doors. There are also two marble graves from the late 14th and early 15th c.

An open staircase from the inner courtyard leads up to the **first floor**. Here can be found the second part of the collection of religious sculpture (Gothic, Renaissance, Baroque); a small collection of dolls and dolls' clothes; lace, coins and medals; chests and caskets; Gothic panels and chasubles (vestments worn at Mass).

The **second floor** houses the "Colleciò Sentimental", a comprehensive collection of small Baroque works of art, tinware, hand tools and various kinds of scales, playing cards, advertisements, dried flowers under

Museu Frederic Marès

BASEMENT

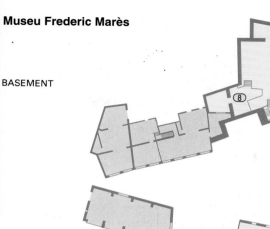

GROUND FLOOR

FIRST FLOOR

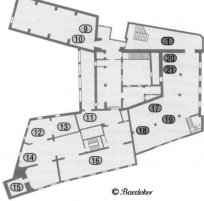

© Baedeker

🔴 **Iberian Culture**

  1 Votive gifts (4th–1st c. B.C.)

🔴 **Classical Antiquity**

  2 Ceres and Proserpha 7; 2nd/3rd c. A.D.)
  3 Roman bronzes (1st c. A.D.)

🟢 **Early Christian Art**

  4 Fragments of sarcophagi (4th c. A.D.)

⚪ **Romanesque**

  5 Madonna (Plantogau 13th c.)
  6 Crucifix (12th c.)
  7 Relief "Calling of St Peter" (12th c.)
  8 Doorway (Anzano, 13th c.)

⚪ **Gothic**

  9 St Peter (Cubells; 14th c.)
  10 Funeral monument (15th c.)
  11 Crucifix (15th c.)
  12 Madonna (Cuéllar, 15th/16th c.)
  13 Polyptchon of St Clara (15th c.)

⚪ **Renaissance**

  14 Adoration of the Shepherds (Relief; 16th/17th c.)
  15 Reliefs from La Espina Monastery (16th c.)
  16 Sculptures and reliefs (Nalda; 16th c.)

⚪ **Baroque**

  17 Head of St Peter (17th c.)
  18 St Peter, Mary Magdalene and Anthony of Padua (17th c.)
  19 St Scholastica (18th/19th c.)
  20 Madonna and Child (18th/19th c.)

🟢 **19th Century**

  21 Bozzetti; clay model for a sculpture

SECOND FLOOR

⬭ Museu Sentimental

1 Montserrat
2 Crib Figures
3 Wrought-iron work
4 Female culture
5 Smokers' utensils
6 Vases
7 Photography
8 Timepieces
9 Ceramics
10 Religious articles
11 Male culture
12 Entertainment

THIRD FLOOR

© Baedeker

glass, scrapbooks, ashtrays, antique cameras, tobacco jars, binoculars, watches, old seals, table silver, porcelain and much more.

Museu i Centre d'Estudis de l'Esport   F 8

Location
Carrer Buenos
Aires 56–58

Metro
Hospital Clínic
(L5)

The Museu i Centre d'Estudis de l'Esport (**Sports Museum** and study centre) is housed in a building dating from the Modernisme period, which was used by Dr Melcior Colet as his consulting rooms and private clinic. In 1982 he made it into a foundation which bears his name and which serves the needs of sport and its cultural importance.

Today the museum houses a variety of exhibitions on various sporting themes (mostly with Catalonian connections). In addition it is the headquarters of a scientific sports research institute.

Open Mon.–Fri. 10am–2pm, 4–8pm.

★★Museu Marítim   I 8–9

Location
Plaça Portal de la
Pau

Metro
Drassanes (L3)

Open Tue.–Sun.
10am–7pm

Near the port (see entry), west of the Columbus Monument, are the striking vaulted buildings with many bays, the form of which clearly betrays their original function. Situated in the docks (Catalan Drassanes), they were once a naval arsenal for the royal fleet. Here has been established the Museu Marítim (**Maritime Museum**) that, after undergoing thorough reorganisation, is one of Catalonia's leading museums.

The shipyard was first built in the 13th c., and by the 18th c. it had been extended to twelve bays. This is where the galleys of the Crown of Aragón were built, serviced and repaired. However, after the discovery of America maritime interests moved to the Atlantic, the importance of the shipyards fell appreciably, and the buildings became used as storage warehouses, powder magazines and military barracks. In 1936 it was

Museu Marítim: history of seafaring in the old shipyard

officially decided to set up a museum here. Since 1976 the whole complex has been under a preservation order. On the southern side, on the Avinguda del Paral·lel, remains of the old town wall have been preserved.

The museum portrays all aspects of the sea and seafaring by means of ships, models of ships, nautical equipment, tools and weapons, diagrams and drawings. Signs guide the visitor on a circular tour.

Rooms 1 and 2 introduce the visitor to the port and royal shipyards of Barcelona, while on the upper floor a number of figureheads and paintings with nautical themes are displayed. Room 6 explores sea-related sports, after which come fishing and shipbuilding and then a most informative exposition on the shift in mankind's view of the world wrought by the voyages of discovery. A large part of the main hall is devoted to Catalonia's overseas links and such themes as colonial policy and emigration (Room 11).

There follows a large-scale multi-media presentation entitled "La Gran Aventura del Mar" ("The Sea – the Great Adventure"), at the entrance to which visitors are supplied with an audio tour relaying a commentary and accoustic effects.

The large exhibition hall is dominated by an excellent life-size replica of the galleon **"Real"**. This was the flagship of the fleet which, under the command of Don Juan d'Austria, defeated the Turks on October 7th 1571 off Lepanto (Greek Naupaktos; south-west Peloponnese) to give Spain mastery of the Mediterranean. The original figurehead, the "Christ of Lepanto", can now be seen in the Cathedral (see entry). The reason for the rebuilding which took place from 1960 onwards was the approaching 400th anniversary of that victory.

From the galleon's upper deck a gangway (good view of the construction of the hall) leads to a large diorama portraying a storm in the Caribbean as experienced from the bows of a sailing ship. Another reconstruction, this time of parts of an ocean-going steamship of about 1900, contrasts shipboard conditions for saloon passengers travelling for pleasure and emigrants crowded together 'tween decks. Finally, a dimly lit section presents an underwater world such as Narcis Monturiol might have observed from his submersible.

The exit is through the caféteria and museum shop, the latter stocking some unusual souvenirs.

Museu Militar

See Montjuïc

★★Museu Picasso   I 10

Location
Carrer Montcada
15–19

Metro
Barceloneta I (L4)

Open Tue.–Sat.
10am–8pm,
Sun. 10am–3pm

On Carrer Montcada, one of the most picturesque of the narrow streets in the Old Town, stands the Palau Berenguer de Aguilar, an imposing Late Gothic palace that now houses the **Picasso Museum**. The collection, arranged in chronological order, includes paintings and drawings as well as prints (lithographs, etchings) from all of Pablo Picasso's artistic periods. The exhibition rooms begin on the first floor; labelling is in two languages (Catalan and Spanish).

Rooms 1–7 contain his early work, and Rooms 8–10 the graphic collection. The artist's early work is strongly influenced by Naturalism and Impressionism. In Room 5 can be found the large painting of "Ciéncia y Caridad", together with his preliminary sketches and studies.

On the second floor Rooms 11–14 are at present closed. Rooms 15–17 house the continuation of his graphic works; Rooms 18 onwards show

A Picasso drawing

paintings arranged in chronological order, with the beginnings of his Cubist period in Room 19. Room 20 is devoted to the "Meninas", a monochrome paraphrase of the work of the same name by Diego Velázquez together with preliminary sketches. Room 21 displays the polychrome version. In Room 22 you can see variations on the theme "Los Pichones" ("The Doves").

On the ground floor are a cafeteria and a large horizontal window which provides a view of a Roman provisions store, with some large two-handled pots.

★Museu Tèxtil i d'Indumentària   I 10

Opposite the Museu Picasso (see entry) stands a 13th c. palace, now the home of the Museu Tèxtil i d'Indumentària (**Textile and Clothing Museum**). It possesses items from the 4th c. AD onwards, as well as from regions inhabited by the Coptics (Egyptians), Moors and from the Christian West.

The ticket office is in the pretty Renaissance inner courtyard, where there is a small display of dolls' clothes and fashion jewellery. The exhibition rooms begin on the first floor, and by following the signs the exhibits will be seen in chronological order. They include finery and sophisticated clothing from the 16th–18th c. as well as many accessories (shoes, handbags, capes); on the walls hang large tapestries. In Room 11 will be found an extensive group of sumptuous 18th c. garments and a display cabinet with shoes; in Room 12 there are similar items from the Empire and Biedermeier periods. Going up one set of stairs brings the visitor to some temporary exhibitions covering specialised subjects, as well as a loom and a model of same.

A little further along the Carrer Montcada, at No. 20, stands the Palau Dalmases, which has been the headquarters since 1962 of the cultural organisation known as the "Omnium Cultural". The 17th c. palace boasts a beautiful inner courtyard with a Renaissance staircase.

Palau Dalmases

The 15th/16th c. Palau Cervelló, on the opposite side of the street at No. 25, is also worth seeing. It houses the **Maeght Art Gallery**.

Palau Cervelló

Location
Carrer Montcada
12–14

Metro
Barceloneta I (L4)

Open Tue.–Sat.
10am–8pm, Sun.,
pub. hols.
10am–3pm

Museu Verdaguer

See Casa-Museu Verdaguer

Nova Icaria   J 13

The site chosen for the Olympic Village (Vila Olimpica) and yachting centre (Port Olimpic) for the 1992 Olympic Games was Nova Icaria, until then a rather dilapidated shoreside industrial zone immediately north of Barceloneta (see entry). With them the city acquired some fine new leisure facilities complete with excellent infrastructure.

The harbour area is dominated by the high-rise buildings of the Hotel Arts Barcelona (one of the city's best and most exclusive hotels) and the company Mapfre.

Location
N of
Barceloneta

Metro
Ciutadella/Port
Olimpic (L4)

Between the tower blocks and the beach extends the spacious new Marina Village, easily identified from afar by its huge emblem, a stylised fish made from interwoven strips of gleaming bronze. The shops in the centre are grouped around surprisingly secluded inner courtyards and water features and sell upmarket clothing, shoes and accessories.

Planet Hollywood, whose opening was attended by Sylvester Stallone, comprises an extravagant mixture of gallery and restaurant.

★★**Marina Village**

A large stylised fish marks the Marina Village in Nova Icaria

Centre of attraction in the glass cube of the entrance area is Arnold Schwarzenegger's Terminator.

The rectangular harbour basin is bounded on the landward side by the Passeig Marítim del Port Olimpic and to the north by the Moll de Carles I. Here there are many good fish restaurants, their terraces affording pleasant views of the harbour.

High above the wide beach of fine sand, running parallel to the main road, is a **promenade** leading to Barceloneta (see entry). There is access to the beach at various points; facilities include bathing, windsurfing (also instruction), boat hire and small bars. Conditions on the beach are monitored, safe bathing or otherwise indicated by coloured flags. Dogs are not allowed.

★★Olympic Stadium

The XXVth Olympic Games opened in Barcelona on July 25th 1992. The Organising Committee's plan envisaged four large arenas spread around the city, all within a radius of some five kilometres (three miles). Only very few competitions took place outside the city area. Existing stadia and halls were used wherever possible, all being completely modernised and extended.

The main venue for sporting events was the extensive Olympic site on Montjuïc (see entry). There is open access to part of the Olympic Stadium. The **Galeria Olimpica** by the south gate is a documentation centre for the Barcelona Games.

Telecommunications tower on the side of the Montjuïc is the new symbol of Barcelona ▶

Palau de Sant Jordi

To the left of the stepped esplanade below the stadium stands the Palau de Sant Jordi, a much admired, single-span sports hall of steel lattice construction. Having excellent acoustics it is now used mainly for concerts. Dominating the entire Olympic site is the modern white telecommunications tower, of distinctive asymmetric design, that has quickly become the city's landmark.

Palau Dalmases

See Museu Tèxtil i d'Indumentària

Palau de la Diputaciò

See Palau de la Generalitat

Palau de la Generalitat   I 10

Location
Plaça Sant Jaume

Metro
Jaume I (L4)

Opposite the Casa de la Ciutat (see entry), on the north-west side of the Plaça de Sant Jaume, the main traffic junction in the Barri Gòtic, towers the former **Palau de la Diputaciò**, built in the 15th c. and once the seat of the medieval body of provincial representatives. Today it houses the Generalitat de Catalunya, the autonomous government of Catalonia.

Well worth seeing is the imposing inner courtyard in the Gothic style; on the first floor is the Chapel of St George, also Gothic. At the back of the building lies the charming orangery.

The inside of the building is open to the public on April 23rd (feast day of Sant Jordi). It is also possible to visit on Saturday or Sunday, but a written request must be made at least fifteen days in advance. For further information about visits, enquire at any local tourist office.

To the north it adjoins the **Audiencia**, once the court house; the Carrer del Bisbe, leading to the cathedral (see entry), is spanned by a charming Gothic building.

★★Palau de la Música Catalana   H 10

Location
Carrer Sant Pere mes alt

Metro
Urquinaona
(L1, L4)

On the north-western edge of the old town, set back a little from the northern side of the Via Laietana, stands the Palau de la Música Catalana (**Palace of Music**); opened in 1908, it is one of the architect Lluis Domènech i Montaner's most unconventional Modernisme designs. Although some extensions have since been added the building still retains its original appearance. The interior, with some 1700 seats, is open to the public only when concerts are held.

This large concert hall displays the full glory of the Catalan Art Nouveau style, with the flowing stucco work and beamed ceilings deserving special mention. It possesses its own chamber orchestra, and performances range from classical to contemporary and experimental music, jazz and pop.

Palau de la Virreina   H–I 9

Location
Rambla 99

Metro
Liceu (L3)

The Palau de la Virreina (**Palace of the Vicereine**) was built between 1772 and 1777 as a residence for Manuel d'Amat i de Junyent, then viceroy in Peru, and named after the vicereine, who continued to live here after his death until 1791. The façade has classical features, while the interior is Late Baroque.

Palau de la Generalitat, seat of the government of Catalonia

Palau de la Música Catalana

Museums

In the past the Museu d'Arts Decoratives (see Palau de Pedralbes) and the Gabinet Postal (Postal Museum) were housed in this palace. The Palau de la Virreina is now home to the Gabinet Numismátic (see entry) and various cultural institutions.

Palau de Pedralbes   D 4

Location
Avinguda
Diagonal
686

Metro
Palau Reial (L3)

Open Tue.–Sun.
10am–2pm

The Palau de Pedralbes lies in the prosperous residential district of similar name (see Pedralbes), close to the Zona Universitaria (see University), in a lovely, well-tended and terraced park with many old cedar and lime trees.

The three-storey building in the Italian style was officially opened on the occasion of the visit in 1924 of the king and queen of Spain. The ground floor with the throne room and adjoining large reception rooms is now used for public functions.

The **gardens** were designed by the Frenchman Jean-Claude Forestier. This was formerly the site of a country house belonging to Count Güell, who then made the land available for the erection of a prestigious royal palace.

★★Museu de Ceràmica

The Museu de Ceràmica, the nucleus of its collection formed by a number of gifts made to the city at the end of the 19th c., has been housed in the Palau de Pedralbes for some years, having previously been accommodated in a museum built specially for the purpose in

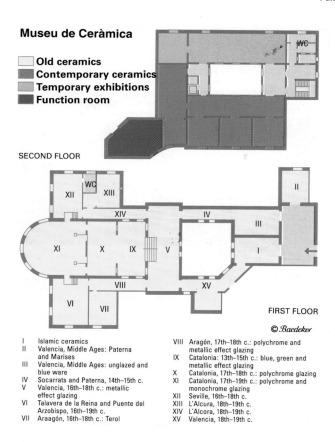

Museu de Ceràmica

- ☐ Old ceramics
- ■ Contemporary ceramics
- ■ Temporary exhibitions
- ■ Function room

SECOND FLOOR

FIRST FLOOR

© *Baedeker*

I	Islamic ceramics	VIII	Aragón, 17th–18th c.: polychrome and metallic effect glazing
II	Valencia, Middle Ages: Paterna and Marises	IX	Catalonia: 13th–15th c.: blue, green and metallic effect glazing
III	Valencia, Middle Ages: unglazed and blue ware	X	Catalonia, 17th–18th c.: polychrome glazing
IV	Socarrats and Paterna, 14th–15th c.	XI	Catalonia, 17th–19th c.: polychrome and monochrome glazing
V	Valencia, 16th–18th c.: metallic effect glazing	XII	Seville, 16th–18th c.
VI	Talavera de la Reina and Puente del Arzobispo, 16th–19th c.	XIII	L'Alcora, 18th–19th c.
VII	Araagón, 16th–18th c.: Terol	XIV	L'Alcora, 18th–19th c.
		XV	Valencia, 18th–19th c.

1931. As clay is one of the most frequently used materials, both in ancient times and nowadays, and fired pottery is moreover extremely durable, the museum offers an excellent insight into cultural history as well as a rich array of aesthetically pleasing objects. Exhibits are arranged according to individual Spanish manufacturers as well as chronologically, the whole blending in well with the backcloth of palace and gardens.

The Historical Department occupies the **first floor** of the palace. In Room 1 are ceramics of Islamic-Spanish provenance.

Rooms 2–5 house a large number of pieces manufactured in Valencia up to the 18th c. (strong Moorish influence; some in metallic-effect glaze). Room 3 contains monochrome blue tiles, some with figural decoration (animals and people), religious symbols, coats of arms and guild marks; Room 5 also has some examples of glazing designed to produce a metallic effect.

Room 6 contains works from Talavera de la Reina (now in the province

The Palau de Pedralbes

of Toledo) and Puente del Arzobispo, dating from the Renaissance to the 19th c. The decoration is partly blue monochrome, partly multi-coloured (animals, people and scenes from everyday life).

Pieces from the ceramic centres of Aragón (from the 13th c. onwards) are displayed in Rooms 7 and 8. Room 7 contains partly monochrome, partly green and blue china; on the wall is a description of the techniques used for colouring (copper oxide for green, manganese oxide for brown and compounds of cobalt for blue). Room 8 houses monochrome and blue and green painted vessels, some having representational decoration, others purely ornamental motifs; a display cabinet on the wall contains a collection of stoups.

Catalonia, which has always produced top quality ceramics, is the source of items displayed in Rooms 9–11. In Room 10 are polychrome and highly ornamental tableware; also of great interest are two large semicircular pictures in glazed tiles depicting a bullfight and a banquet in a prosperous middle-class house. The semicircular Room 11 is noted for its display of glazed tiles showing skilled craftsmen at work as well as animal and everyday scenes.

The Islamic tradition lingered on, especially in Seville, as late even as the Renaissance. In Room 12, glass display cabinets on the wall contain long friezes recounting a complete story.

In 1727 a new factory was established in Alcora (now in the province of Castellón de la Plana) to manufacture European-style ware (Rooms 13 and 14).

Polychrome ceramics from Valencia (19th c.), predominantly the popular decorated tiles known as "azulejos" (from the Arabic "az-zuleyche, meaning mosaic, not, as was once assumed, the Spanish "azul", meaning blue), are exhibited in Room 15.

The **second floor** houses the Department of Contemporary Ceramic Art, some items here being traditional or with epigonic decoration based on older patterns, but the majority avant-garde. The spacious cabinets in the last room contain pieces by Joan Miró and Pablo Picasso. Temporary exhibitions are also frequently held on this floor.

The museum possesses an educational department, a ceramic workshop and a specialist library.

Museu d'Arts Decoratives

The Museu d'Arts Decoratives (**Museum of Arts and Crafts**) occupies the rooms facing the Museu de Ceràmica (see above). The chronologically arranged collection comprises furniture and applied art from the Romanesque period to the present day. Note the Gothic chests, some elaborately painted, also the particularly magnificent Renaissance escritoires and writing cabinets, richly inlaid with intarsia in mother-of-pearl, ivory and different coloured woods. There are fine examples of Baroque, Empire and Neo-Classical furniture, and a contemporary section featuring Jugendstil, Art Nouveau and Noucentisme furniture and accessories; the closer to the present day, the more evident the influence of industrial design.

The Finca Güell (see entry) borders the park to the north-east.

Palau Episcopal   I 10

The Palau Episcopal (**Episcopal Palace**) in the Barri Gòtic adjoins the cathedral (see entry) on the west. It was first recorded as long ago as 926; the oldest parts of the present building date from the 12th, 13th and 15th c. Restoration work was carried out in 1883 and again in 1928. The two round towers on the Portal del Bisbe date from Roman times. The inner courtyard, with its Romanesque arcades, contains a modern statue of Our Lady from the Montserrat (see entry).

Location
Plaça Nova

Metro
Liceu (L3)
Jaume I (L4)

★Palau Güell   I 9

In 1886 the architect Antoni Gaudí was instructed by his patron, Eusebi Güell, to build an high-status residence on a plot of land measuring only 18 × 22 m (60 × 73 ft), on the Carrer Nou de la Rambla, a narrow street in the old town.

Eusebi Güell was a great patron of the arts, and he wished to see this reflected in the palace: in the very centre of the building a large domed hall – intended to be used for poetry readings and private concerts – extends from the first floor right up to the roof. Around it are grouped the living rooms; the ground floor, which opens on to the street through two parabolic portals with artistic wrought-iron grilles bearing the letters E and G, Eusebi Güell's initials, housed the stables. The entire building reflects Güell's enormous wealth, with its sumptuous décor, valuable textiles and individually designed furniture, most of it by Gaudí. Here, perhaps more than in any other building, we see the ostentatious – today perhaps almost comical – imagination of the master architect. Even the roof was not forgotten when it came to art, as the dome and chimney – like those on the Casa Milà – come across as elements of decorative sculpture.

Location
Carrer Nou de la
Rambla 3–5

Metro
Drassanes, Liceu
(L3)

Open Mon.–Fri.
4–8pm;
closed pub. hols.

The Museu d'Art Escènic, from which the present Museu de les Arts de l'Espectacle (**Museum of Performing Arts**) has developed, was moved to the Palau Güell in 1954. It contains costumes, stage sets, models, theatrical notices and documents, some dealing with the Realistic School of Catalan dramatic art and some with ballet, and manuscripts and personal memorabilia relating to important actors and actresses. There are

**Museu de les Arts
de l'Espectacle**

temporary exhibitions drawn from the rich fund of special material owned by the museum. There is also a specialist library.

The museum is at present undergoing reorganisation and is closed to the public.

Palau Moja

See Eglesia de Betlem

★★Palau Nacional   H–I 5

Some distance from the Plaça d'Espanya (see entry), above the Exhibition Grounds (see entry), at the top of a wide flight of steps, stands the giant domed and architecturally somewhat over-ornate Palau Nacional (**National Palace**), which has been the home of the Museum of Catalan Art since 1934. The palace, originally built for the World Exhibition of 1929, has recently had its interior completely renovated by the Italian architect Gae Aulenti. On the entrance level are a huge auditorium with a large organ and a museum shop.

Location
Mirador del Palau Nacional

Bus
61 from Plaça Espanya

★★Museu Nacional d'Art de Catalunya

The Museu Nacional d'Art de Catalunya (MNAC; **Museum of Catalan Art**), with its splendid collections covering the history of Catalan art, is one of the most-important places to visit in Barcelona. This museum is currently being remodelled and may be in parts or wholly closed.

Open Tue.–Sat. 10am–7pm, Sun., pub. hols. 10am–2.30pm

The world-ranking Department of **Romanesque Art** (11th–13th c.) is particularly impressive. Here can be seen magnificent frescos from many churches in the Pyrenean region of Catalonia. For this purpose, vaulted ceilings and apses from the original sites have been exactly reproduced with the wall paintings incorporated in them, while faithful copies of the originals have replaced them in the churches from which they were taken. Photographs, ground plans and drawings of the churches concerned accompany the exhibits. Highlights of the collection are the strongly coloured frescos from the apses in the churches of Sant Climent and Santa Maria in Tahull. Note also the liturgical articles, altarpieces, column capitals and sculptured figures.

The Department of **Gothic Art** (14th and 15th c.) is partly arranged systematically rather than chronologically. Its collections are not limited to Catalonia, but also include works from other regions of Spain. On display are wooden and stone sculptures, panel paintings and altarpieces (including a massive 14th c. altar to Our Lady by members of the Serra family of artists who worked in Barcelona between 1357 and 1405.

The relatively small **Renaissance Baroque** department contains items from other areas of Spain as well as from the Spanish Netherlands.

Jardins Maragall

Opposite the main entrance to the Palau Nacional lie the impeccably maintained gardens known as the Jardins Maragall (named after the Catalan poet Joan Maragall i Gorina, 1860–1911), in which stands the **Palau Albeniz**, built in 1929 and with murals by Salvador Dalí. As the palazzo is now used to provide accommodation for state visitors it is not often open to the public.

◄ *Wall painting in the Palau Nacional: Christ in Majesty*

Parc de la Ciutadella   I 11–12

Location
Passeig Picasso/
Passeig de
Pujades

Metro
Barceloneta,
Ciutadella (L4)

The Parc de la Ciutadella (**Citadel Park**) is a large green space covering some 30 ha (75 acres) on the north-eastern edge of the Old Town. It was laid out on the site of the razed citadel, which Philip V had built to suppress the rebellious population and to safeguard the harbour district. Here can be found pathways, flower-covered terraces, waterfalls and monuments. One of the park's most pleasant attractions is the "Umbracle", a structure of brick and wood with the interior filled with tropical plants. As well as museums and the zoo, some local government offices (including the **Parlament de Catalunya**) are situated here.

On the south-western edge, along the Passeig Picasso, stand the **Hivernacle**, a large glazed iron building dating from the turn of the 19th c. (recently restored and used for exhibitions and cultural events), the Museu de Geologica, the Museu de Zoologica (see entries), and the **Palm House**.
In 1988, the centenary of the 1888 World Exhibition, a statue of A. Clavé was erected in the basin of a fountain behind the Zoological Museum.

Right at the rear of the park you will come to the ostentatious **Cascade**, supplied by a canal and containing a number of allegorical figures and gargoyles in the form of animals. In front of it stands the Music Pavilion and a large statue of a mammoth pointing to the nearby Zoo (see entry).

Museum d'Art
Modern

See entry

Parc de l'Espanya Industrial   G 5

Location
Carrer del Rector
Triado

Metro
Sants-Estació
(L3, L5)

The large Sants railway station is the terminus for all trains to the south. Here are situated the Expo Hotel and the dominating Torre Catalunya. The Plaça Països Catalans to the north-east has been designed in a rather unfortunate modern manner, and because of its large metal roof it has been disparagingly nicknamed the "gasolinera" ("petrol station"). However, the Parc de l'Espanya, to the south-east of the railway station, fits quite well into its modern surroundings.

Spaced-out seats of natural stone also serve as steps down to a small artificial lake and canal, where boats can be hired; a number of towers with floodlighting stretch as far as the eye can see. Some very young trees are growing in the lawns, and there are courts for squash and basketball. A roomy multi-purpose sports hall caters for a range of other activities. Children adore sliding on the large metal dragon situated at the park entrance.

★★Parc del Laberint   A 14–15

Location
N of the
Passeig de la Vall
d'Hebron

Metro
Montbau (L3)

On the north-west edge of the city lie the modern residential suburbs of Montbau and Vall d'Hebron. In 1992 the neighbourhood acquired an added attraction when the Velòdrom (cycle-racing track) was constructed for the Olympic Games.

Buses operate a free shuttle service between the Metro station and the Hospital de Sant Miquel. From the bus stop at the entrance to the hospital grounds it is just a few steps past the velodrome to the very attractive and peaceful Parc del Laberint.

The Parc de l'Espanya Industrial near the main station

The Fountain Pavilion in the Parc de Laberint

In 1791 Count Antoni Desvalls began laying out a park at his country seat, which at that time lay well outside the city boundary. He entrusted the task to an Italian, a French and two Catalan architects, who between them designed gardens in the Neo-Classical and early Romantic styles around an existing 14th c. tower.

The park extends across the flank of a hill, and with its dense, lush vegetation and abundance of pools, water channels and cascades is extremely impressive. Signs guide visitors on a tour which takes in the grottoes with figures from Greek mythology, the labyrinth (which gives the park its name), a Neo-Classical fountain pavilion, and a mock cemetery laid out for purely decorative purposes, finally arriving back at the entrance gate.

In early summer (Jun.–Jul.) classical music concerts are held in the park.

★Parc Güell   D 11–12

Location
Carrer Olot

Metro
Lesseps, Vallcarca
(L3)

Open daily
10am–dusk

In the Vallcarca district of the city, between Eixample and Tibidabo (see entries), on the side of a hill lies Parc Güell, laid out between 1900–14. It was designed by Antoni Gaudí, who also had his house here. The rather difficult climb can be avoided by taking the escalator on the right of the Avinguda de l'Hospital (to the north-west of the Lesseps metro).

Along the south-eastern wall (Carrer Olot) some brightly coloured majolica medallions spell out the name of the park. Close by the entrance, with its beautiful iron gate, is a porter's house built in a fluid style, decorated with a tower and largely covered in coloured majolica. Close by is a small bar. This is at the bottom of a twin set of symmetrical steps leading up to a hall with columns. It is divided by a fountain, with the main emphasis on a brightly coloured salamander-like animal in majolica.

The columned hall to which the steps lead displays elements of the Greek Doric style; the outside rows of columns lean noticeably inwards, to counteract the sideways force exerted by the vaulted roof. Between the capitals of the rather gloomy and archaic-looking columns can be seen some rich polychrome decoration made of ceramic and glazed mosaics.

On the roof of this hall a wide, flat area has been laid out, the surrounding wall of which forms a long, wavy seat. This curved wall results in a number of individual, enclosed conversation seats. Here visitors can observe the original decoration of multi-coloured ceramic fragments which completely covers the seats. The terrace offers a panoramic view of the city and the sea.

In the park are a number of other features designed by Gaudí: colonnades, viaducts and grottoes.

Casa Museu Gaudí

Open May–Sep.
daily 10am–8pm;
Mar., Apr., Oct.
7pm; Nov.–Feb.
6pm

The house in which Antoni Gaudí lived from 1906 to 1925 stands in the middle of the park. It has been converted into a museum containing some original drawings, items from the estate and the like.

Parc Joan Miró   G 6

Location
Carrer de
Tarragona

Metro
Plaça d'Espanya
(L1, L3)
Tarragona (L3)
"Dona i Ocell"

Where the abattoir (escorxador) once stood is now the Parc Joan Miró (also known as Parc de l'Escorxador).

The park lies on two levels. The larger (lower) part adjoins the bullring (see Plaça de Toros, Les Arenes); it has many rows of palm trees, together with bowling greens and football pitches.

The higher part of the park is completely paved and has a square pond in which stands the statue "Dona i Ocell" ("Woman with Bird"), covered in multi-coloured ceramic fragments, the work of Joan Miró in 1983.

Modernisme details ...

... in the Parc Güell

★★Passeig de Gràcia   F–H 10

Location
Plaça de
Catalunya to
Plaça
Joan Carles I

The Passeig de Gràcia is undoubtedly the most elegant and striking boulevard in the Eixample (see entry). It links the Plaça de Catalunya (see entry) on the edge of the old town with the Gràcia district to the north-west adjoining the Eixample, where it continues as the much narrower Carrer Gran de Gràcia.

Along this broad street, flanked with rows of trees, will be found numerous banks and quality shops; note in particular the many stately houses built in the Modernisme style, which give it its characteristic stamp.

The typical greenish-grey relief stones used in the pavement were designed by Antoni Gaudí.

The arms of the Catalonian capital occur frequently in the many artistic wrought-iron candelabra.

The Passeig de Gràcia forms the main axis through the Quadrat d'Or (see entry), which was the upper-class residential area around the turn of the 19th c.

Casa Milà

See entry

Casa Batiló

See entry

Museu de la
Música

See entry

★Pavellò Mies van der Rohe   H 5

Location
Avinguda del
Marquès de
Comillas

Metro
Plaça d'Espanya
(L1, L3)

Shortly before the road from Poble Espanyol (see entry) reaches the Exhibition Grounds it passes the Pavellò Mies van der Rohe.

Ludwig Mies van der Rohe, born in 1886 and the last director of the famous Bauhaus in Dessau (Germany), designed the German Pavilion for the World Exhibition in Barcelona in 1929, and on the centenary of his birth this replica of the original pavilion was dedicated to his memory. The building's severe lines and the aesthetic effect of the materials used (glass, steel, polished natural stone) are very effective; within stands a statue of Georg Kolbe. The chairs in the pavilion were designed as the "Barcelona" model for the World Exhibition and still retain their timeless elegance.

There is also a documentation centre which works in close co-operation with the Mies van der Rohe Archives in the Museum of Modern Art in New York.

Pedralbes   C 3–D 4

Location
W of the city
centre

Pedralbes is one of the most favoured residential areas of Barcelona; the more modern of the University (see entry) buildings are also grouped in the Zona Universitaria.

Metro
Maria Cristina,
Palau Reial, Zona
Universitaria (L3)

The king of Spain himself resides here, in the Palau de Pedralbes (see entry). The main place to visit in this suburban district, once a village and later absorbed by Barcelona, is the convent near the end of the Avinguda de Pedralbes.

★Monestir de Pedralbes

Railway station
(FGC)
Reina Elisenda

The Monestir de Pedralbes is a convent of the Order of St Clare, founded in 1326 by Queen Elisenda de Montcada. In front of it lies the small park known as the Jardines Reina Elisends, with cypress trees and native shrubs. The church and convent buildings are very similar in style.

Open Tue.–Sun. 10am–2pm; closed pub. hols.

Pavelló Mies van der Rohe

From the park a doorway in the left-hand wall of the nave leads to the interior of the Gothic **church**, lined with chapels. The broad interior is divided into two by a wall and wrought-iron screen; only one side is open to the general public, the other being reserved for the convent community. Note the 15th c. stained-glass windows and the alabaster tomb of Queen Elisenda (d. 1364), the wife of James II.

The three-storey **cloister** with its pretty Renaissance fountain is likewise only partly open to the public. It is best to go round in an anticlockwise direction. On the right is the Capella de San Migues, with paintings (1346) by Ferran Bassa evidently strongly influenced by contemporary Italian art. Next come several so-called day cells and access to the refectory, kitchen and sickbay. The refectory is a rather austere room with admonitory Latin inscriptions and biblical quotations on its walls. The infirmary consists of a suite of smaller rooms each with 6 to 8 beds. The kitchen with its picture tiles is also of interest.

Stairs descend from the cloister to the domestic offices and storerooms; in the **Sala Joan Mari i Oliva** are a sequence of 21 small, carefully crafted dioramas depicting scenes from the Life of Christ.

Displayed in rooms off the cloister is a collection of liturgical items, illuminated manuscripts and a wooden model of the monastery complex. In the **inner courtyard** stand palms and cypresses and a quite delightful Renaissance fountain surrounded on four sides by benches with majolica decoration.

Since 1993 part of the world-famous ★★ **Thyssen-Bornemisza art collection** has been exhibited in the monastery. The lower level of the cloister leads to the former Dormitorium, a large room spanned by projecting vaulting. Hanging here are some 80 central European paintings of pre-

The Plaça de Catalunya forms the northern end of the Ramblas

dominantly religious content dating from the Middle Ages to the Venetian Baroque.

See entry	Palau de Pedralbes
See entry	Finca Güell

Pedrera

See Casa Milà

★Plaça de Catalunya   H 9–10

The busy Plaça de Catalunya forms the north-western end of the inner-city Ramblas (see entry) and also of the core of the old town. A number of large banks are situated around this wide and spacious square; the north-west side is dominated by the Banco Espanōl de Crédito building, while on the east side stands the massive Telefónica (Telephone Exchange) edifice.

Metro
Catalunya (L1, L3)

    Below the level of the square, and with entrances from several sides, lies the city's principal Metro junction; in addition, the trains covering the city routes (e.g. the FGC to Tibidabo, Pedralbes and Sant Cugat del Vallés; see entries) run from here.

The square and particularly the Metro station beneath it are a favourite haunt of pickpockets and tricksters.

Advice

◀ *The peaceful Monestir de Pedralbes*

On the northern side of the square stands the large department store **El Corte Inglés**, known for its large selection of regional goods and which is certainly worth a visit. It has an interpreter service linked to the internal telephone system, to assist foreign customers in making their purchases. On the ninth floor is a large self-service restaurant with a terrace through the windows of which there is a fine view over the centre of the city; a pause here is recommended as a pleasant break from touring Barcelona. Open Mon.–Sat. 10am–9pm.

Plaça del Rei

See Museu d'Història de la Ciutat

Plaça d'Espanya   G–H 5

Metro
Plaça d'Espanya
(L1, L3)

The circular Plaça d'Espanya, with a continuous flow of vehicles passing round it, is the main traffic junction in the west of the city. This is where the Gran Via de les Corts Catalanes (usually known as "Gran Via" for short), which cuts straight across the whole of the city, and the Avinguda de la Paral·lel, which skirts the foot of Montjuïc (see entry), intersect. In the centre of the open space stands the lavish memorial fountain "España Ofrecida a Dios" ("Spain dedicated to God").

On the southern side the entrance to the Exhibition Grounds (see entry) is formed by two towers modelled on the bell towers of St Mark's in Venice, and on the north stands the large round Plaça de Toros (Les Arenes; see entry).

★Plaça Reial   I 9

Location
Ramblas

Metro
Drassanes, Liceu
(L3)

The Plaça Reial (not to be confused with Plaça del Rei; see Museu d'Història de la Ciutat) is connected with the Rambla dels Caputxins (see Ramblas) by a short diagonal road (Carrer Colom). This beautiful square is enclosed by houses in the Classical style, the ground floors of which include arcades with shops and restaurants.
 The square was laid out in the middle of the 19th c. on the site of a former Capuchin monastery. Among palm trees in the centre stands the beautiful Fountain of the Three Graces; the candelabra was designed by Antoni Gaudí.
 In recent years the square has increasingly become the haunt of drug addicts. Not even a permanent police presence, aimed chiefly at preventing violence, has noticeably improved the situation.

Plaças de Toros   G 6 and G 12–13

Location
Gran Via de les
Corts Catalanes

Barcelona possesses two bullrings (known as Plaças de Toros or Plaças de Braus). One, "Les Arenes" (Gran Via 385), adjoins the Plaça d'Espanya, while the other, "La Monumental", lies at the north-eastern

Plaça Reial in the Old Town

end of the Gran Via (No. 747) and the Plaça de les Glóries, where Gran Via and the Diagonal cross.

The wide, circular **Arenes**, 52 m (172 ft) in diameter, and with seats for some 15,000 spectators, was built around 1930. No bullfights are held here nowadays. You should note the large butterfly made from multi-coloured china mosaics on the front of the "Casa de la Papallona" near the arena (architect: Josep Graner i Prat).

The **Monumental** is the only ring where bullfights ("corridas") are still held. It also has a bullfighting museum.

For general information about bullfighting see Introduction, Customs. For season and times see Practical Information, Bullfights.

Planetarium   C 7

As well as the one in the Museu de la Ciència (see entry) Barcelona has another planetarium in the Carrer de les Escoles Pies. By means of complicated projection apparatus practically every conceivable phenomenom and constellation in the heavens can be portrayed. Computer technology facilitates impressive audio-visual displays. Demonstrations (Mon.–Fri. 9.30, 10.30 and 11.30am, 3, 4 and 5pm, Sun. and pub. hols. noon, 1.30 and 6.30pm) are accompanied by expert commentary.

Location
Carrer de les
Escoles Pies 103

Railway station
(FGC) Sarrí

★★Poble Espanyol   H 4

In the western part of the extensive parkland on Montjuïc (see entry) is the Poble Espanyol (**Spanish Village**), laid out for the 1929 World Exhibition, it displays the building styles which are typical of the various

Location
Avinguda Marquès
de Comillas

123

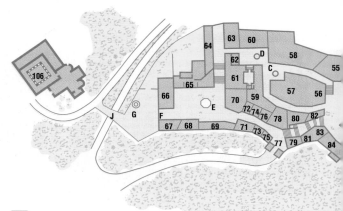

 Craft shops

 (20)
Information

 (5) (34)
Toilets

 (104) (34)
Bureau de change

 (20)
Lost property

 (5) (20) (34)
Telephone

 (2)
First Aid

 (19)
Museum

 (72)
Museum

 (2)
Tobacconist

 (9)
Administration

ORIGINAL LOCATIONS OF BUILDINGS, REPLICAS OF WHICH ARE IN THE "SPANISH VILLAGE"

1 Avila
2 Cáceres
3 Miajadas (Cáceres)
4 Plasencia
5 Cáceres
6 Sigüenza (Guadalajara)
7 Sigüenza (Guadalajara)
8 Navalcarnero (Madrid)
9 Santillana de Mar (Santander)
10 Borja (Zaragoza)
11 Riaza (Segovia)
12 Santillana del Mar (Santander)
13 Alquézar (Huesca)
14 El Burgo de Osma (Soria)
15 El Burgo de Osma (Soria)
16 Aranda de Duero (Burgos)
17 Sigüenza (Guadalajara)
18 Cambados (Pontevedra)
19 Cáceres
20 Cáceres
21 La Fresneda (Teruel)
22 La Fresneda (Teruel)
23 Sangüesa (Navarra)
24 Graus (Huesca)
25 Jérica (Castellón)

26 Montblanch (Tarragona)
27 Sigüenza (Guadalajara)
28 Segovia
29 Toledo
30 Valderrobres (Teruel)
31 Cambados (Pontevedra)
32 Cambados (Pontevedra)
33 San Esteban de Lorenzana (Lugo)
34 Medinaceli (Soria)
35 Maluenda (Zaragoza)
36 Betanzos (La Coruña)
37 Betanzos (La Coruña)
38 Caldas de Reyes (Pontevedra)
39 Cangas de Onis (Oviedo)
40 Morella (Castellón)
41 Molinos de Duero (Soria)
42 Calaceite (Teruel)
43 Catí (Castellón)
44 Jérica (Castellón)
45 Peñafiel (Valladolid)
46 Sariñena (Huesca)
47 Fraga (Huesca)
48 Borja (Zaragoza)
49 Albarracín (Teruel)
50 Albarracín (Teruel)

SPANISH VILLAGE

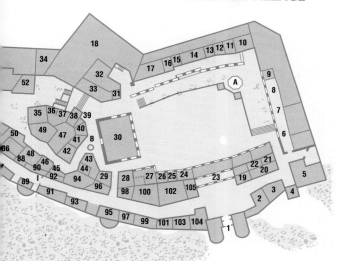

A San Mateo: Musikpavillon
B Catí: Brunnen
C Tarifa: Brunnen
D Córdoba: Virgen de los Faroles
E Prades: Brunnen
F Prades: Puerta de Prades
G Ulldecona: Wegkreuz
I Maya: Torbogen
J Ribes de Fresser

51 Corella (Navarra)
52 Alcañiz (Teruel)
53 Torralba de Ribota (Zaragoza)
54 Utebo (Zaragoza)
55 Ronda (Málaga)
56 Arcos de la Frontera (Cádiz)
57 Córdoba und Sevilla
58 Ecija (Sevilla)
59 Córdoba
60 Ubeda (Jaén)
61 Murcia
62 Córdoba
63 Arcos de la Frontera (Cádiz)
64 Mallorca
65 La Jana (Castellón)
66 Tárrega (Lérida)
67 Cornudella (Tarragona)
68 La Gárriga (Barcelona)
69 Santa Pau (Girona)
70 Besalú (Girona)
71 Rupit (Barcelona)
72 Rupit (Barcelona)
73 Isona (Lérida)
74 Montblanch (Tarragona)
75 Rupit (Barcelona)
76 Camprodón (Girona)
77 Montblanch (Tarragona)
78 Montblanch (Tarragona)

79 Besalú (Girona)
80 Rupit (Barcelona)
81 Belianes (Lérida)
82 Morella (Castellón)
83 Santa Pau (Girona)
84 Vitoria
85 Vergara (Guipúzcoa)
86 Estella (Navarra)
87 Erandio (Vizcaya)
88 Roncal (Navarra)
89 Maya (Navarra)
90 Olazagutia (Navarra)
91 Vinuesa (Soria)
92 Molinos de Duero (Soria)
93 Vinuesa (Soria)
94 Sos del Rey (Zaragoza)
95 Toro (Zamora)
96 Toro (Zamora)
97 Segovia
98 Toro (Zamora)
99 Santillana del Mar (Santander)
100 Burgo de Osma (Soria)
101 Ayllón (Segovia)
102 Ayllón (Soria)
103 Sigüenza (Guadalajara)
104 Cáceres
105 Torija (Guadalajara)
106 Monasterio (Girona)

Poble Espanyol

Poble Espanyol: the main square ...   *... and a picturesque inner courtyard*

Metro
Plaça d'Espanya,
then bus 61

Open Mon.
9am–8pm, Tue.,
Wed., Thu.
9am–2pm, Fri.,
Sat. 9am–4pm,
Sun.
9am–midnight

provinces of Spain. Many well-known artists were involved in choosing, modelling and planning the layout.

The Poble Espanyol numbers among the most popular places to visit in Barcelona. As in most Spanish country towns, the houses are grouped around the main square, the "plaça major", near the massive entrance gate. Near the entrance are information kiosks, the branch of a bank, book and souvenir shops. Open-air events are also held here from time to time.

West of the main square lie a number of picturesque streets and alley-ways, with glimpses of some beautiful little courtyards. A surprisingly large number of craftworkers have been established here and offer for sale some fine examples of their art; glass, ceramics, enamel-work, textiles, leather goods, prints and so on will be found in colourful abundance and at reasonable prices. Visitors are usually welcome to look around the workshops.

The village is now owned by a private company and has been extensively renovated. A new entertainment centre was added in 1988 with bars, restaurants, clubs and a theatre tent, as well as a children's theatre. A popular attraction is the "Barcelona Experience", an audio-visual presentation of the city with commentary in English (through headphones).

Museu d'Arts, Indústries i Tradicions Populars

Just through the entrance gate, to the right in Carrer de la Conquesta, we come to the Museu d'Arts, Indústries i Tradicions Populars (**Museum of The Arts, Industry and Popular Traditions**). It is a branch of the Museu Etnològic, containing its Spanish and Catalan departments. Tours by arrangement; tel. 934236954.

Museu del Llibre i de les Arts Gràfiques

The Poble Espanyol also incorporates the Museu de les Arts Gràfiques

(**Museum of Graphic Art**). On display are wood and metal relief plates, old printing presses, and various examples of textual and graphic printing. Tours by arrangement; tel. 934261999.

★Port   K 1–J 10

The port (Port Franc de Barcelona), with its outer harbour of about 300 ha (740 acres), occupies the whole of the coastal strip between the district of Barceloneta (see entry) and the southern foothills of Montjuïc (see entry). Before Spain showed renewed interest in the Atlantic and her possessions in Central and South America in the 17th c., the port of Barcelona was one of the most influential in the Mediterranean, and even today ranks as the most important in the whole of Spain. The northern part of the harbour area and the section of coast that lies beyond Barceloneta were redesigned and rebuilt in an ambitious project in 1992.

Location
E of the
city area

Metro
Barceloneta (L4),
Drassanes (L3)

The merchant port extends from the foot of Montjuïc, from which it is separated by the broad Cinturó del Litoral (an arterial road leading to the airport and on to Tarragona). With the ports of Gijón and Bilbao it is the most modern in Spain; the annual volume of traffic is about 18 million metric tons. The main imports are oil, coal, wheat and cotton; first and foremost among its exports are wine, olive oil and cork.

For tourists, by far the most interesting part of the port is the north-eastern section. The Moll de Barcelona, which borders it to the south, is the landing place for passenger and ferry boats travelling to the Balearic Islands of Mallorca, Menorca and Ibiza.

★★Columbus Monument

At the Plaça del Portal de la Pau stands the Monument a Cristòfor Colom (Columbus Monument), 60 m (197 ft) high and weighing 205 metric tons, erected for the World Exhibition in 1888. The iron column is completely covered with allegorical figures. Around the base is a series of reliefs depicting important stages in Columbus's life and voyages of discovery. On the top of the column is an 8-m (26-ft) statue of Columbus, which points out to sea (and therefore not directly towards the New World). A lift takes visitors up to an observation area from where there are excellent views of the port and the city. On the windows transparent pictures and captions serve to facilitate the visitor's orientation.

At the foot of the monument, in the Portal de la Pau, horse-drawn carriages offer tours of the area.

South of the monument stands the imposing and rather ornate customs building (Duana).

Anchored here until a short time ago was a replica of the "Santa Maria", Columbus's flagship on his first expedition to America. It was apparently destroyed by arsonists.

Moll de la Fusta

The Moll de la Fusta is the name given to the section of the port between Portal de la Pau and the Plaça d'Antoni Lòpez. The Moll de Bosch i Alsina, which runs directly parallel, and is linked to it by two draw-bridges, has been transformed into a spacious promenade with seats, restaurants and an underground car park. Along the Moll the **Golondrinas** ("swallows") landing-stage can be reached, from where boat trips round the port may be taken (duration approximately 30 minutes).

View of the port from Montjuïc

The Rambla del Mar leading to the Maremagnum

Port Vell

From the Columbus Monument proceed past the Port Authority building to the **Rambla del Mar**, a wide, pedestrians only, pontoon bridge across the mouth of the Old Harbour. It leads to the Moll d'Espanya which has been turned into a vast leisure centre with a large underground car park; only the Reial Club Maritime survives from the days before the redevelopment.

Moll d'Espanya

The Maremagnum, a massive building of concrete, metal and darkened glass, houses innumerable food outlets, retail shops, boutiques and galleries as well as a large amusement arcade called "Big Fun". On the roof, surrounded by terrace restaurants, there is a minigolf course. For sheer extravagance it would be hard to beat the "Dive", a restaurant with an interior like a submarine straight out of a fantasy film; it was designed by Steven Spielberg, the US film director.

★**Maremagnum**

Adjacent to the Maremagnum is a **cinema complex** (Cines Maremagnum) with an eight-theatre multiplex cinema and IMAX.

The main attraction on the Moll d'Espanya is the aquarium, said to be the largest of its kind in Europe. Marine animals and plants from all the world's oceans can be observed in numerous salt-water tanks reaching almost to the height of a room. The most remarkable exhibit is a submarine landscape with sharks, moray eels and sunfish, and a sunken ship carrying amphorae; it is used to demonstrate the methods of underwater archaeology. Visitors pass right through the tank in two glass tunnels.

★★**Aquarium**

Open daily from 9.30

In front of the Aquarium stands a replica of the submarine "Ictineo II"

From the aquarium a flight of steps leads up to the rotunda, where there is a very well presented and informative exhibition on the theme of the sea as a highway for trade and cultural exchange. It covers the period from the 2nd/1st c. BC and is reinforced with displays and video sequences.

Ictineo II

Near the north end of the Old Harbour basin stands a replica of Narcis Monturiol's wooden submarine "Ictineo II", launched in Barcelona in 1859 and in which Monturiol made a total of 54 dives to depths of 20 m (65 ft). The replica was constructed for the 1993 film "Monturiol, Senyor del Mar".

★★Harbour cable car

Spanning the harbour basin diagonally is the harbour cable car (in Catalan "Transbordador Aerí"; operating times – weekdays noon–6.45pm, Sun. and public holidays 11.30am–8pm). The harbour terminus is the Torre de Sant Sebastian on the new mole, a 96 m (315 ft) steel lattice mast (the Plaça del Mar with sports and cultural facilities is planned); the intermediate station is the 158 m (519 ft) Torre de Jaume I on the Moll de Barcelona. The funicular ends on the north-east side of Montjuïc (see entry), near the Jardins Mossen Costa i Llobera (cactus garden). During the journey passengers can enjoy a splendid view of the port area and the wide Passeig de Colom.

Maritime Museum

See Museu Marítim

Olympic harbour

See Nova Icaria

★★Quadrat d'Or   F–H 9–11

Location
Between the Old Town and the Diagonal

Metro
Catalunya (L1, L3), Passeig de Gràcia (L3, L4), Diagonal (L3, L5)

See plan p. 131

"Quadrat d'Or" ("Golden Quarter") is the name given to that area of the Eixample (see entry) containing the best and most numerous examples of the Modernist style of architecture. It is bordered mainly by the Plaça de Catalunya to the south, by the Avinguda de la Diagonal to the north, by the Passeig de Sant Joan to the north and Carrer Muntaner to the south-west. The main road through it is the Passeig de Gràcia (see entry).

What gives the Quadrat d'Or its special charm is the large number of well-preserved late 19th and early 20th c. residences designed by a number of different architects and thus providing a varied cross-section of the Modernist style. Literally at every step the visitor will stumble across interesting details – ceramic art, stained glass windows, wrought-iron work, reliefs, mosaics, statues and much more besides – a genuine "open-air" museum.

★★Ramblas   H–I 9

Location
Between Barri Gòtic and Barri Xino

Metro
Catalunya (L1; also FGC), Drassanes, Liceu, Catalunya (L3)

The Rambles (here better known under the Catalan name "Ramblas"), the principal thoroughfare in the city centre, stretches north-westward from the Columbus Memorial near the Port (see entry). The 1180-m (3870-ft) section to the Plaça de Catalunya (see entry) is lined with plane trees; with its wide pedestrian zone flanked by a narrow road on each side it is a favourite place for a stroll, and is one of Barcelona's main attractions. To the right (north-east) lies the Barri Gòtic, to the left (south-west) near the Barri Xino (see entries). As well as the flower and bird market the Ramblas boasts a considerable number of book and news-paper stands, and restaurants and cafés with tables in the open. The pavement artists, street musicians and other impromptu performers all add to its distinctive atmosphere; but be warned against getting

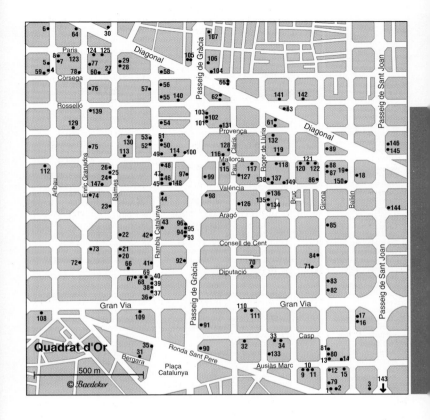

1 Casa Victorià de la Riva
  Carrer Ali Bei 1
  Enric Sagnier i Villavecchia
2 Casa Modest Andreu
  Carrer Ali Bei 3
  Telm Fernàndez i Janot
3 Cases Joaquim i Antoni Marfà
  Carrer Ali Bei 27–29
4 Casa Joaquim Cairó
  Carrer Aribau 149 bis
  Domènech Boada i Piera
5 Casa Conrad Roure
  Carrer Aribau 155
  Ferran Romeu i Ribot
6 Cases Pascual i Cia
  Carrer Aribau 175–177
  Antoni Millàs i Figuerola

7/8 Casa Societat Torres
  Germans
  Carrer Aribau 178
  Jaume Torres i Grau
9/10 Cases Manuel Felip
  Carrer Ausiàs Marc 22
  Roc Cot i Cot
11 Casa Antonia Puget
  Carrer Ausiàs Marc 22
  Roc Cot i Cot
12 Cases Francesc Borés
  Carrer Ausiàs Marc 30–32
  Francesc Berenguer i Mestres
13 Cases Antoni Roger
  Carrer Ausiàs Marc 33–35
  Enric Sagnier
  i Villavecchia

14 Cases Tomas Roger
  Carrer Ausiàs Marc 37–39
  Enric Sagnier
  i Villavecchia
15 Casa Antònia Borès
  Carrer Ausiàs Marc 46
  Juli Batllevell i Arús
16 Casa Francesc de Paula Vallet
  Carrer Bailén 36
  Gabriel Borell
  i Cardona
17 Casa Jaume Sahis
  Carrer Bailén 48
  Joesp Pérez i Terraza
18/19 Casa Rossend Capellades
  Carrer Bailén 126
  Jeroni Grandell i Manresa

Quadrat d'Or

20/21 Cases Josep J. Bertrand
Carrer Balmes 44–50
Enric Sagnier i Villavecchia
22 Cases Antoni Miquel
Carrer Balmes 54
Jeroni Granell i Manresa
23 Casa Jeroni Granell
Carrer Balmes 65
Jeroni Granell i Manresa
24 Cases Joan Pons
Carrer Balmes 81
Joan Pons i Traball
25 Casa Jaume Larcegui
Carrer Balmes 83
Eduard Mercader i Sacanell
26 Cases Frederic Vallet Xiró
Carrer Balmes 85–87
Josep Maria Barenys
i Gambús
27 Casa Josep Filella
Carrer Balmes 149
Manuel J. Raspall i Mayol
28 Casa Francesc Fargas
Carrer Balmes 156
Francesc Fargas i Margenat
29 Cases Adolf Ruiz
Carrer Balmes 158–160
Adolf Ruiz i Casamitjana
30 Casa Lluís Pérez Samanillo
Carrer Balmes 166–169
Joan Hervas i Arzimendi
31 Casa Emilia Carles de Tolrà
Carrer Bergara 11
Emili Sala i Cortès
32 Casa Llorenç Camprubi
Carrer Casp 22
Adolf Ruiz i Casamitjana
33 Casa Antoni Salvadó
Carrer Casp 46
Juli Batllevell i Arús
34 Casa Calvert
Carrer Casp 48
Antoni Gaudi
35 Casa Bosch i Alsina
Plaça de Catalunya 8
Joaquim Bassegoda i Amigó und
Pere Bassegoda i Mateu
36 Casa Pia Batlló
Rambla de Catalunya 17
Josep Vilaseca
i Casanovas
37 Casa Heribert Pons
Rambla de Catalunya 19–21
Alexandre Soler i March
38 Casa Jaume Moysi
Rambla de Catalunya 23
Manuel Comas i Thos
39 Casa Sebastià Ptatjusà
Rambla de Catalunya 27
Antoni Serra i Pujals
40 Casa Climent Asols
Rambla de Catalunya 25
Francesc del Villar i Carmona
41 Casa Rodolf Juncadella
Rambla de Catalunya 33
Enric Sagnier i Villavecchia
42 Casa Miquel A. Fargas
Rambla de Catalunya 47
Enric Sagnier i Villavecchia
43 Casa Dolors Calm
Rambla de Catalunya 54

Josep Vilaseca i Casanovas
44 Casa Bonaventura Pollés
Rambla de Catalunya 72
Bonaventura Pollés i Vivó
45 Casa Asunción Belloso de
Gabriel
Rambla de Catalunya 74
Josep Doménech i Estapà
46/47 Casa Evarist Juncosa
Rambla de Catalunya 76
Salvador Viñals i Sabaté
48 Casa Francesc Farreras
Rambla de Catalunya 86
Josep Pérez i Terrasa
49 Casa Josep i Ramón Queraltó
Rambla de Catalunya 88
Josep Plantada i Artigas
50 Casa Pilar Albiñana de
Regàs
Rambla de Catalunya 92–94
Francesc Berenguer
i Mestres
51 Casa Ferran Cortés
Rambla de Catalunya 96
Enric Sagnier i Villavecchia
52/53 Casa Manuel Verdú
Rambla de Catalunya 101/103
Maurici Augé
54 Casa Dolors Vidal de Sagnier
Rambla de Catalunya 104
Enric Sagnier i Villavecchia
55 Cases Godó-Lallana
Rambla de Catalunya 112
Josep Majó i Ribas
56 Casa Antonia Costa
Rambla de Catalunya 122
Josep Doménech i Estapà
57 Casa Llorenç Armengol
Rambla de Catalunya 125
Adolf Ruiz i Casamitjana
58 Casa Serra
Rambla de Catalunya 126
Josep Puig i Cadafalch
59 Casa Antoni Piera
Casser Córsega 239
Domènech Boada i Piera
60 Casa Pau Martí
Carrer Córsega 271
Domènech Boada i Piera
61 Casa Pilar Bassols
Avinguda Diagonal 355
Gabriel Borrell i Cardona
62 Palau Baró de Quadras
Josep Puig i Cadafalch
63 Casa Terrades (Casa
Punxes)
Avinguda Diagonal 416/420
Josep Puig i Cadafalch
64 Casa Miquel Sayrach
Avinguda Diagonal 423/425
Manuel Sayrach i Carreras
65 Casa Comalat
Avinguda Diagonal 442
Salvador Valeri i Pupurull
66 Casa Josep J. Bertrand
Carrer Diputació 235/237
Enric Sagnier i Villavecchia
67 Casa Clapès
Carrer Diputació 246
Joaquim Bassegoda i Amigó
68 Casa Miquel Ibarz

Carrer Diputació 248
Salvador Soteres i Taberner
69 Casa Rupert Garriga Nogués
Carrer Diputació 250
Enric Sagnier i Villavecchia
70 Casa Marcel li Costa
Carrer Diputació 299
Architect unknown
71 Casa Josep Fabra
Carrer Diputació 329
Enric Sagnier i Villavecchia
72 Casa Antoni Pàmies
Carrer Enric Granados 5
Melcior Viñals i Muñoz
73 Casa Domenech i Estapà
Carrer Enric Granados 20
Joseph Domènech i Estapà
74 Casa Leandre Bou
Carrer Enric Granados 20
Antoni Serrallach
75 Casa Anna Salvadó de Guitart
Carrer Enric Granados 48
Josep Coll i Vilaclara
76 Casa Adolf Ruiz
Carrer Enric Granados 94
Adolf Ruiz i Casamitjana
77 Casa Francesc Cairó
Carrer Enric Granados 106
Domènech Boada i Piera
78 Casa Enric Llorens
Carrer Enric Granados 119
Josep Pérez i Terraza
79 Casa Enric i Voctòria de la Riva
Carrer Girona 4
Enric Sagnier i Villavecchia
80 Casa Antoni Roger
Carrer Girona 22
Enric Sagnier i Villavecchia
81 Casa Enric Roger
Carrer Girona 24
Enric Sagnier i Villavecchia
82 Casa Ramon Vilà
Carrer Girona 46
Joan Maymó i Cabanellas
83 Casa Jacinta Ruiz
Carrer Girona 54
Ramon Viñolas i Llossas
84 Casa Esperança Isern
Carrer Girona 67
Roc Cot i Cot
85 Casa Isabel Pomar
Carrer Girona 86
Joan Rubió i Bellver
86 Casa Eduardo de Lamadrid
Carrer Girona 113
Lluís Domènech i Montaner
87 Casa Adolf Ruiz
Carrer Girona 120
Adolf Ruiz i Casamitjana
88 Casa Jeroni Granell
Carrer Girona 122
Jeroni F. Granell i Manresa
89 Casa Francesc Cairó
Carrer Girona 132
Domènech Boada i Piera
90 Cases Pons i Pasqual
Passeig de Gràcia 2/4
Enric Sagnier i Villavecchia
91 Cases Antoni Rocamora
Passeig de Gràcia 6–14
Joaquim Bassegoda i Amigó

92 Casa Manuel Margarida
    Passeig de Gràcia 27
    Joaquim Codina i Matali
93 Casa Lleó Morera
    Passeig de Gràcia 35
    Lluis Domènech i Montaner
94 Casa Ramon Mulleras
    Passeig de Gràcia 37
    Enric Sagnier i Villavecchia
95 Casa Amatller
    Passeig de Gràcia 41
    Josep Puig
    i Cadafalch
96 Casa Batlló
    Passeig de Gràcia 43
    Antoni Gaudí
97 Casa Alexandre i Josefina
    Jofre
    Passeig de Gràcia 65
    Bonaventura Bassegoda
    i Amigó
98 Casa Marfà
    Passeig de Gràcia 66
    Manuel Comas i Thos
99 Casa Joan Coma
    Passeig de Gràcia 74
    Enric Sagnier
    i Villavecchia
100 Casa Enric Batlló
    Passeig de Gràcia 75
    Josep Vilaseca i Casanovas
101 Casa Milà (La Pedrera)
    Passeig de Gràcia 92
    Antoni Gaudí
102 Casa Josep Codira
    Passeig de Gràcia 94
    Antoni Rovira i Rabassa
103 Casa Ramon Casas
    Passeig de Gràcia 96
    Antoni Rovira i Rabassa
104 Casa Rupert Garriga
    Passeig de Gràcia 112
    Enric Sagnier
    i Villavecchia
105 Casa Bonaventura Ferrer
    Passeig de Gràcia 113
    Pere Falques i Urpi
106 Casa Lluis Ferrer-Vidal
    Passeig de Gràcia 114
    Eduard Ferrés i Puig
107 Casa Fuster
    Passeig de Gràcia 132
    Lluis Domènech
    i Montaner
108 Casa Jeroni Granell
    Gran Via 582
    Jeroni F. Granell i Manresa
109 Casa Josep Portabella
    Gran Via 616
    Domènec Balet i Nadal
110 Casa Camil Mulleras Garrós
    Gran Via 654

    Enric Sagnier i Villavecchia
111 Casa Ramon Oller
    Gran Via 658
    Pau Salvat i Espasa
112 Cases Jeroni Granell
    Carrer Mallorca 184–188
    Jeroni F. Granell
    i Manresa
113 Casa Gustau Peyra
    Carrer Mallorca 235
    Enric Sagnier
    i Villavecchia
114 Casa Angel Batlló
    Carrer Mallorca 253–257
    Josep Vilaseca
    i Casanovas
115 Casa Marqués de Julià
    Carrer Mallorca 264
    Enric Sagnier
    i Villavecchia
116 Cases Amadeu Maristany
    Carrer Mallorca 273/275
    Bonaventura Bassegoda
    i Amigó
117 Palau Ramon de Montaner
    Carrer Mallorca 278
    Lluis Domènech
    i Montaner
118 Casa Francesc Farreras
    Carrer Mallorca 284
    Antoni Millàs i Figuerola
119 Casa Thomas
    Carrer Mallorca 291/293
    Lluis Domènech i Montaner
120/121 Cases Dolors Xiró de Vallet
    Carrer Mallorca 302/304
    Josep Barenys i Gambús
122 Casa Carme Carsi de Puig
    Carrer Mallorca 306
    Josep Barenys i Gambús
123 Casa Societat Torres Germans
    Carrer París 182
    Jaume Torres i Grau
124 Casa Josep Batlles
    Carrer París 202
    Francesc Ferriol i Carreras
125 Casa Teresa Vallhonrat
    Carrer París 204
    Francesc Ferriol i Carreras
126 Casa Rafael Barba
    Carrer Pau Claris 140/142
    Enric Sagnier i Villavecchia
127 Cases Leandre Bou
    Carrer Pau Claris 154/156
    Antoni Millàs i Figuerola
128 Casa Dolors Xiró de Vallet
    Carrer Pau Claris 161
    Josep Barenys i Gambús
129 Casa Segarra
    Carrer Provença 185
    Josep Masdeu i Puigdemasa
130 Casa Francesc Pastor

    Carrer Provença 258
    Enric Sagnier i Villavecchia
131 Casa Josep Ferrer-Vidal
    Carrer Provença 267/269
    Enric Sagnier i Villavecchia
132 Casa Francesc Lalame
    Carrer Provença 324/326
    Arnau Calvet i Peyronill
133 Cases Joaquim Cabot
    Carrer Roger de Llúria 8–14
    Josep Vilaseca i Casanovas
134 Casa Pere Salisachs
    Carrer Roger de Llúria 72
    Salvador Viñals i Sabaté
135 Casa Agustí Anglora
    Carrer Roger de Llúria 74
    Isidre Raventós i Amiguet
136 Cases Castillo Villanueva
    Carrer Roger de Llúria 80
    Juli Fossas I Marinez
137 Casa Jaume Forn
    Carrer Roger de Llúria 82
    Jeroni F. Granell i Manresa
138 Casa Jeroni Granell
    Carrer Roger de Llúria 84
    Jeroni F. Granell i Manresa
139 Casa Esteve Recolons
    Carrer Rosselló 192
    Pere Bassegoda i Mateu
140 Casa Baldomer Rovira
    Carrer Rosselló 247
    Andreu Audet i Puig
141 Casa Leonor Matas
    Carrer Rosselló 293
    Jeroni F. Granell i Manresa
142 Casa Alexandre Gioan
    Carrer Rosselló 301
    Ramon Ribera i Rodriguez
143 Casa Enric Laplana
    Passeig Sant Joan 6
    Bernardi Martotel i Puig
144 Casa Eulàlia Artés de Mayolas
    Passeig de Sant Joan 84 bis
    Salvador Viñals i Sabaté
145 Casa Macaya
    Passeig de Sant Joan 108
    Josep Puig i Cadafalch
146 Casa Dolors Alesan de Gibert
    Passeig Sant Joan 110
    Enric Fatjó i Torras
147 Casa Marti Llorens
    Carrer València 213
    Antoni Alabern i Pomar
148 Casa Domènech i Estapà
    Carrer València 241
    Josep Domènech i Estapà
149 Casa Pau Ubarri
    Carrer València 293
    Moquel Madorell i Rius
150 Casa Manuel Llopis
    Carrer València 339
    Antoni Galissà i Soquè

involved in any games of chance. It is also unfortunately true to say that pickpockets and tricksters find rich pickings here.

The newly constructed **Rambla del Mar** (see Port, Port Vell) now provides a link between the Columbus Monument and the Moll d'Espanya with its wide range of entertainment and leisure facilities.

Rambla de Santa Monica

Near the Columbus Monument (see Port) is the start of the Rambla de Santa Monica. Right at the beginning of the street, on the left, lies the Naval Command Headquarters; a few steps further, at the corner of the Portal de Santa Madrona, is the **Centre d'Art Santa Monica**, with some high quality temporary art exhibitions, and the parish church of the same name. The Waxworks (see Museu de Cera) lies on the other side of the Rambla.

Rambla dels Caputxins

From the Rambla dels Caputxins the Carrer Nou de la Rambla branches off on the left; here stands the Palau Güell (see entry). An opening on the right leads to the Plaça Reial (see entry). A few steps further, on the same side of the street, is the Carrer Ferran Jaume I, the shortest route to the Barri Gòtic. Further left stands the Gran Teatre del Liceu (see entry). The Rambla dels Caputxins ends at the Plaça de la Boqueria; from here the Carrer del Cardenal Casanyas leads northwards to the church of Santa Maria del Pí (see entry).

Rambla dels Flors (Rambla de Sant Josep)

On its north-western side the Plaça del Boqueria adjoins the Rambla de Sant Josep. This is where the colourful flower market is held each morning, and which has given it its popular name of the "Rambla dels Flors". On the left side are the market hall (see Mercat de Sant Josep), and the Palau de Virreina (see entry). At the junction of the Rambla and the Carrer del Carme looms the sombre and heavy façade of the Eglesia de Betlem (see entry), once the Jesuit church.

Rambla dels Estudis

At the junction with the Carrer del Carme is the beginning of the Rambla dels Estudis, where the bird and fish market is held in the mornings. Together with the **Rambla Canaletes** it forms the link with the Plaça de Catalunya (see entry).

Rambla de Catalunya

The north-western extension of the Ramblas forms the far side of the square known as the Rambla de Catalunya, which stretches from the Eixample (see entry) to the Avinguda de la Diagonal. It has none of the flair and atmosphere of the old Ramblas, being on a par with all the other purely functional routes through the new part of the city.

★★Sagrada Família — G 12

The Sagrada Família church (officially known as "Temple Expiatori de la Sagrada Família", the **Holy Family Church of the Atonement**), is the most famous sight in Barcelona and also one of Europe's most unconventional churches. Dominating its surroundings, it stands in the northern part of the city.

When Antoni Gaudí was put in charge of constructing the church in

Location
Plaça Gaudí

Metro
Sagrada Família
(L5)

◀ *The Ramblas: a favourite place for strolling*

Temple de la Sagrada Família

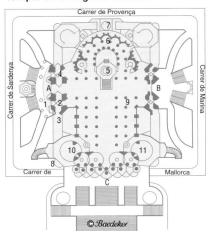

Carrer de Provença
Carrer de Sardenya
Carrer de Marina
Carrer de
Mallorca
© Baedeker

A Doorway of the Passion
B Christmas Doorway
   (over the above the towers
   of the façade)

1 Entrance
2 Vestibule
3 Model of church
4 Sales kiosk
5 Altar (crypt below)
6 Apse
7 Lady Chapel
8 Gaudí Museum
9 Model Workshop
10 Baptistry
11 Chapel of the Sacrament

Open summer
9am–8pm; spring,
autumn until
7pm; winter until
6pm

1883 plans had already been drawn up and some work done on building the crypt of what was to be a purely Neo-Gothic church. Gaudí decided to change the plans completely but – as in the case of most of his other works – had no firm ideas in mind, preferring to alter and add to the plans as work progressed. This meant that there was no question of getting it built quickly, although Gaudí had originally forecast between ten and fifteen years; there were also financial limitations, as the cost was to be met solely from alms and public subscription. As a result the "Church of the Poor", the main work by the most important Catalan architect of the 20th c., remains just a shell, and nobody knows whether and when it will ever be completed.

The church is planned to have a total length of 110 m (354 ft) and a height of 45 m (148 ft), with a principal dome of 160 m (525 ft) and towers up to 115 m (378 ft). So far, however, only the four-towered east façade (the "Nativity Front"), the outer walls of the apse, the crypt in which Antoni Gaudí was buried in 1926 (not open to the public), parts of the west doorway (the "Passion Doorway"), and the nave walls have been built.

From an artistic point of view the Temple de la Sagrada Família is an extremely unconventional mixture of established styles and new ideas. The ground plan, the way the area is divided up, and the fine lines strongly reflect Gothic and mid-19th c. Neo-Gothic, but are combined with the flowing, herbaceous ornamentation so typical of the Art Nouveau style.

Recently work on the main crypt that houses the **museum** has restarted, and it is expected that the range of exhibits will also change.

The present entrance is in the leftmost crypt near the entrance, where postcards are sold. Of interest are the sketches and photographs illustrating Gaudí buildings and of the ancient ones on which they are modelled. In separate departments can be seen plaster mock-ups of the sculptured decoration; there is also a large, partially restored model of the church that was shown in Paris in 1910. The studies covering the

Temple de la Sagrada Família ▶

Sagrada Família

The towers of the Sagrada Família

window and façade designs clearly illustrate the principle of "diagonal supports" that Gaudí wished to see replace the Gothic buttress. Also of interest is a wire model illustrating structural engineering principles; Gaudí hung weights on an inverted wire framework to represent the anticipated stresses and strains, thus showing clearly the static base structure. To understand it fully you have to imagine the picture turned through 180 degrees.

At the end of the crypt is a large photographic reproduction of the Passion Façade; to its right is the iconography, in the Catalan dialect, of the individual motifs. There is also a multi-video show, and in one of the side rooms a model cut in half to show the nave and side aisles.

The first doorway, the west or **Passion Doorway**, has been added to in recent years. There is a striking difference in styles between the sculpture forms (by José Maria Subirach) used here and the other decoration influenced by Gaudí. Note the portrayal of Christ wearing a veil; it is in bas-relief and produces the optical illusion that the head is moving closer to the observer.

Through the entrance stands the large plaster model of the church (scale 1:25), showing the Passion Façade; here too are a number of water-colours of the other fronts and doorways.

The broad **interior** is still a building site with several cranes; prefabricated building sections give a realistic idea of the form it will take. Where the transepts and apse meet stands the altar protected by a canopy, under which lies the main crypt (where Antoni Gaudí was interred in 1926; normally closed).

The **towers** of the right side doorway (Nativity Doorway) can be climbed, but the open, narrow winding staircase makes it a rather unattractive proposition for anybody prone to giddiness. Nearby is an aged lift; it is worthwhile going up in this to enjoy the fantastic **view** over the city and of the helm roofs of the towers, clad in colourful majolica, reminiscent of bishops' mitres.

The small building nearby with the undulating roof, once the builders' hut, is now used as offices and is not open to the public.

Santa Anna   H 9

In a narrow street a little to the east of the Plaça de Catalunya (see entry) stands the **Convent of Santa Anna**, founded in the 12th c. by the Order of the Holy Sepulchre and dissolved in 1835. The cloister and chapter house, both of which still remain, were built in the 15th c.; many other parts from the same period were pulled down in the 19th c.

Originally Romanesque in style, the church has a cruciform ground plan and rectangular choir. The interior has round arches and was partially altered in the 14th c.; its small Romanesque windows provide little light. The tabernacle is a copy of the 15th/16th c. original, which has long since disappeared.

The 14th c. Chapel of the Blessed Sacrament lies to the left of the entrance. In it will be found some modern paintings and a 15th c. burial group.

From the church there is access to the cloister and thence to the chapter house.

Location
Carrer
Rivadeneyra

Metro
Catalunya (L1, L3)

Santa Maria del Mar   I 10

On the Carrer Montcada, a little way south of the Museu Picasso (see entry), stands the church of Santa Maria del Mar (1329–83), a Gothic edifice without transepts. After the cathedral (see entry) it is the most important ecclesiastical building in the city. It occupies the site of a Late Roman necropolis where, according to legend, St Eulalia was buried.

A large rose window opens above the richly decorated main door; the sumptuous interior gives an harmonious impression of space. Most of the stained glass dates from the 15th–17th c.; in the chapel near the left side door can be seen a black madonna. Note also the stone bosses in the vaulting; the Coronation of Our Lady is depicted above the main altar. On the main altar stands a Gothic statue of the Madonna, and in front of it a model of an old trading ship. Below the raised chancel is the entrance to the crypt.

The small square on the right of the church is taken up by a **memorial**, sunken after the manner of an amphitheatre. On the long walls of polished natural stone is a dedication to the Catalans who died in battle against the troops of Philip V in 1714.

Location
Plaça Montcada

Metro
Jaume I (L4)

★Santa Maria del Pí   I 10

On the little Plaça del Pí in the old town stands the Gothic church of Santa Maria del Pí (**Our Blessed Lady of the Pine Tree**). The otherwise rather sober main façade is relieved by an arched doorway with a Gothic statue of the Madonna and by a large rose window. The main tower and those on the front have no domes.

The plain interior is flanked by chapels. The clerestory possesses stained-glass windows from the 15th to the 18th c., while those in the rose window are copies of the originals that were destroyed in 1936. Near the door to the sacristy lies the Gothic tomb of Arnau Ferre, who died in 1394 at the siege of Catania in Sicily.

The treasury contains gold and silversmith work and other sacred art.

Location
Plaça del Pí

Metro
Liceu (L3)

Plaça de Sant Josep Oriol

The left-hand wall of the nave adjoins the pretty, shady Plaça de Sant Josep Oriol, with some attractive shop entrances. Under the trees in the middle of the square stands a memorial to the poet and dramatist Angel Guimerá i Jorge (1845–1924).

The Plaça del Pí (see above) leads to a glass-roofed shopping precinct with several streets crossing it; in the **Barri del Pi**, where it widens out, are a number of art, antique and jewellery shops.

Sant Cugat del Vallès

Excursion
15 km (9½ mi.) NW

Railway station
(FGC)
Sant Cugat

The little town of Sant Cugat del Vallès lies some 15 km (9½ mi.) north-west of Barcelona. The best road goes via Valvidrera; more scenic, but narrower and winding, is the alternative road via the Tibidabo (see entry). A rail connection from the Plaça de Catalunya (see entry) can be made with the trains of the FGC.

Monastery

Open Mon., Wed.,
Fri. 10am–noon
(church); Tue.–Sat.
10am–2pm,
4pm–7pm
(cloister)

The first documented record of the former Benedictine monastery was in 897; the present Romanesque–Gothic edifice dates from the 12th–17th c. and is therefore not unified in style. The cloister area, so steeped in atmosphere, is still largely walled.

The main front of the aisled church is relatively low and stocky with a plain Gothic doorway, dominated by a large rose window above and two smaller ones at the side. The choir section, with a main apse and two side apses, is Romanesque, but with a plain tracery window in the former. Also Gothic are the stump of the central tower and the windows in the side aisles. Inside can be seen a beautiful Altar to the Blessed Sacrament (1375) and the tomb of Abbot Odo (14th c.).

On the left of the church front is the entrance to the cloister. Note in particular the 150 or so capitals decorated with figures.

Sant Pau del Camp   I 8

Location
Carrer Sant Pau

Metro
P'ral·lel (L3, L3)

The church of Sant Pau del Camp (**St Paul-in-the-Field**) owes its name to the fact that it was built outside the town boundary within the fields. The Avinguda de la Paral·lel now runs through here, forming the boundary between the old town (see Barri Xino) and the new development at the foot of Montjuïc (see entry).

Sant Pau del Camp is a Romanesque building dating from 1117, on a cruci-form ground plan with a triple-domed choir and a massive central tower. Note the beautiful main door, with its marble capitals from the later Gothic period.

The groin-vaulted interior adjoins the Gothic chapter house on its right, which in turn leads out into the cloister.

★Stock Exchange   I 10

The Stock Exchange (Catalan **Llotja**) was founded in the 14th c. when the city was at its economic zenith. Nothing has remained of the first building, which was erected close to the shore. The present Stock Exchange was built between 1380 and 1392 in the Late Gothic style, but was then extended and altered in the 15th, 16th and 18th c., the last such additions being in the classical manner that characterises the exterior of the building. Until a few years ago the Academy of Art (Escola de Belles Arts) was also situated here.

The only part of the Stock Exchange which has not been changed since its inception is the elegant **Gothic Room**, an aisled room divided by arches resting on slender columns, in which even today the business of the Stock Exchange is still conducted. Also of note are the staircase with its allegories of industry and trade and the purely classical rooms of the Junta de Comerç (chamber of trade) on the upper floor.

The square adjoining the Stock Exchange to the north (Pla del Palau) is the focal point of Barcelona's maritime trade. Around it are grouped numerous offices and commercial and administrative buildings, including the Govern Civil (civil administration).

Further north and to the right hand side is the Estació de França, the "French Railway" (with rail connections to the north). On the occasion of the Olympic Games it was extensively renovated, along with the surrounding area and now, behind its historic façade, conceals the most up-to-date transport and communication technology.

Location
Pla del Palau

Metro
Barceloneta (L4)

Pla del Palau

Estació de França

Temple de la Sagrada Família

See Sagrada Família

★★Tibidabo   A 9

To the north-west of the city centre rises Tibidabo, 532 m (1746 ft) high and one of the most popular tourist destinations in the Barcelona district. It derives its name from the legend which says that it was here that Christ was tempted by the devil with the words "I will give you ...", the Latin for which is "tibi dabo ...".

From the Plaça de Catalunya visitors can travel by the underground railway (Ferrocarrils de la Generalitat) as far as the Avinguda del Tibidabo terminus. From here there is a nostalgic trip by tram, known as the **"Tramvia Blau"** because of its blue-painted coaches (note: these may be temporarily replaced by public buses), up the hill as far as the funicular cableway station for the final lap to the top. The lower station of the cableway is 223 m (732 ft) above sea level, with a restaurant and a model of the Tibidabo. A road, 8 km (5 mi.) long, also winds its way from the city up the hill.

Location
NW of the
city centre

Railway station
(FGC)
Avinguda del
Tibidabo,
then by bus or
Tramvia
Blau (Blue Tram)
and cableway

Sagrat Cor

On the top of Tibidabo stands Sagrat Cor church (**Church of the Sacred Heart**), built on various levels as recently as 1961 in Gothic style by the architect Enric Sagnier. The ground floor is a building strongly reminiscent of the period around the turn of the century; in the apse a mosaic portrays people dressed in clothes worn by middle-class citizens of the time.

On the second level stands the basilica, Neo-Gothic in style and almost circular in plan; its enormous height gives the impression of great spaciousness.

A lift goes up to a platform 542 m (1778 ft) above sea level, with several towers.

Steps lead to the ambulatory round the foot of the giant statue of Christ, which can be seen from miles away. From here there is a superb **view** of Barcelona and the sea, over the chain of mountains which includes Tibidabo and the wooded hills of the interior. To the south stands a TV mast used for transmitting the Olympic Games, and to the north the transmitters of Radio Barcelona and Catalunya Radio.

In the Parc d'Atraccions on Tibidabo

Tibidabo
Parc d'Atraccions

A–H Refreshments
I   Toilets, Telephone
L   Souvenirs

1 Pan-o-ramic	8 Montaña Rusa	15 Piratta	22 Alaska
2 Atalaya	9 Pasaje del Terror	16 Viking	23 Tibidabo Express
3 Roundabout	10 Miralls Màgics	17 Tchu-Tchu-Tren	24 Barka Choke
4 Rodeo	11 Museo Autómatas	18 Zoochok	25 Castillo
5 Tibi-Air	12 Treping	19 Tralla	Misterloso
6 Tibi-Bobs	13 Galaxy	20 Aladino	26 Funicular
7 Mini-Congo	14 Crash-Cars	21 Diavolo	

From the cable railway station on the hill a small train takes tourists to
the 228 m (748 ft) Torre de Collserola (built in 1990). Strict security checks
have to be undergone before entering the lift up to the viewing platform
136 m (446 ft) above the ground. The platform, the sides and even
bottom of which are completely glazed, has information boards with
directions and distances to assist orientation. The view is magnificent.

★★**Torre de
Collserola**

★Parc d'Atraccions

Most visitors to Tibidabo head for the Parc de Atraccions, an amusement park constructed on several levels on the steep mountainside,

similar to that on the Montjuïc (see entry). Dating from 1901 the amusement park has recently been renovated. There are various types of rides (roller coaster, big wheel, dodgems, go-carts) and other amusements, games of skill, computer games, several restaurants and so on. Families with children will find a visit to the park particularly worthwhile; it is best to plan to spend at least half a day there or, better still, a full day, when the visit can be combined with a visit to the Museu de la Ciència (see entry) near the lower station of the Tramvia Blau.

As well as the normal entry ticket – which is comparatively cheap but only includes six determined attractions – there is an "all-in" ticket that includes the use of all the facilities at no extra cost. The hours of opening vary but can be obtained from any tourist office.

**Museu
d'Autómates**

Tucked in among the other attractions in the amusement park is the Museu d'Autómates, a collection of old gaming machines, jukeboxes, mechanical dolls and model railways.

Triumphal Arch

See Arc de Triomf

University   G 9 and D–E 3–4

As early as the end of the 13th c. the Dominican monks in Barcelona provided educational facilities in the form of a "Studium Generale", and in 1401 institutions were established for the study of medicine and the fine arts, theology, law and philosophy being added a little later. However, following the annulment by Philip V of the special privileges granted to Catalonia, the academy was closed down in 1717. It was 1837 before teaching returned to Barcelona.

At present the University of Barcelona has some 58,000 registered students. For further information on higher education in the city see Introduction, Culture.

From the southern corner of the Plaça de Catalunya the busy shopping street of Carrer del Pelai continues westward to the Plaça de la Universitaria. Here stand the buildings of the **Old University**, constructed between 1863 and 1873 in a neo-Romanesque style. Inside can be seen two beautiful atriums and parts of the university library.

Some way out, at the south-western end of the Avinguda de la Diagonal, the extensive modern campus of the **Zona Universitaria** spreads over the Pedralbes (see entry) district of the city. It is here that the faculties of the natural, social, and economic sciences of the university are situated.

Waxworks

See Museu de Cera

★Zoo   I 11–12

The Zoo was founded in 1892, and covers some 14 ha (35 acres) of the eastern part of the Parc de la Ciutadella (see entry). An astonishing amount of skill and imagination has gone into creating such a varied layout in the smallest of spaces.

Very well laid out are the reptile house and, in particular, the aquarama (dolphinarium), which also houses a giant killer whale, *Orcinus orca*. The circular pool is surrounded by the two-storey aquarium, with salt water on the upper level and fresh water below; the dolphinarium can be viewed through reinforced glass.

The bird house with a separate section for nocturnal birds is also well designed.

There are a number of refreshment stalls and picnic tables, some near the centrally located model of Montserrat (see entry). The skeleton of a large whale is on display. It is easy to find the way around, as there are coloured symbols on all the pathways indicating the various sections.

Original in concept is the well-known statue of the "Senyoreta del Paraigua" ("Lady with the Umbrella").

Metro
Ciutadella (L4)

Open daily
10am–5pm
in winter;
9.30am–7.30pm
in summer

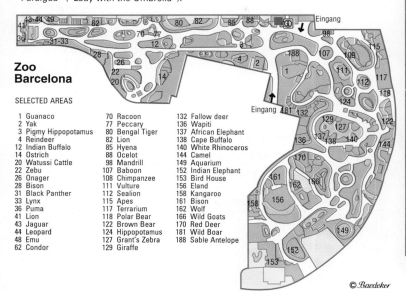

Zoo
Barcelona

SELECTED AREAS

1 Guanaco	70 Racoon	132 Fallow deer
2 Yak	77 Peccary	136 Wapiti
3 Pigmy Hippopotamus	80 Bengal Tiger	137 African Elephant
4 Reindeer	82 Lion	138 Cape Buffalo
12 Indian Buffalo	85 Hyena	140 White Rhinoceros
14 Ostrich	88 Ocelot	144 Camel
20 Watussi Cattle	98 Mandrill	149 Aquarium
22 Zebu	107 Baboon	152 Indian Elephant
26 Onager	108 Chimpanzee	153 Bird House
28 Bison	111 Vulture	156 Eland
31 Black Panther	112 Sealion	158 Kangaroo
33 Lynx	115 Apes	161 Bison
36 Puma	117 Terrarium	162 Wolf
41 Lion	118 Polar Bear	166 Wild Goats
43 Jaguar	122 Brown Bear	170 Red Deer
44 Leopard	124 Hippopotamus	181 Wild Boar
48 Emu	127 Grant's Zebra	188 Sable Antelope
62 Condor	129 Giraffe	

© Baedeker

**Practical
Information
from A to Z**

Air Travel

Airport

Barcelona Airport is situated about 10 km (6 mi.) south-west of the city in El Prat de Llobregat, close to the motorway (C244) to Castelldefels. RENFE, the state railway company, operates connecting services to the city centre (Sants station; stopping at El Clot, Arc de Triompf, Plaça de Catalunya and Sants Estació) every 30 minutes between 7am and 11pm, journey time 25 minutes. There are also buses (lines EA and EN to the Plaça d'Espanya) and taxis.

Airlines

British Airways
Passeig de Gràcia 85
E–08008 Barcelona
Tel. 932156900

Iberia
Plaça d'Espanya
E–08007 Barcelona
Tel. 933257358; Infoiberia 902400500

Most other airlines serving Barcelona have desks at the airport.

Bullfights

In Barcelona bullfights are held on almost every Sunday and public holidays from Easter to November and sometimes also on weekdays (particularly Thursdays). They take place between 4 and 6 or between 5 and 7 in the afternoons, but only in good weather. During the dog days (July–August) and from mid-October onwards only the lesser forms of bullfighting, known as *novilladas*, with less experienced bullfighters and young bulls, are held.

For further information on bullfighting see Introduction, Customs and Traditions.

The bullring Plaça de Toros Monumental is situated south-west of the Plaça de les Glòries Catalanes.

Camping

More than two-thirds of all Spanish campsites are situated in the autonomous region of Catalonia and here they are concentrated in the area near the coast. The equipment of the sites is considerably above the average for the country; the sites are divided officially into four categories designated L (luxury), 1, 2 and 3.

Every campsite provides safe keeping for articles of value; it is advisable to deposit with them large sums of money and valuables.

In the case of justified complaints the visitor should demand the *Hoja de Reclamaciones*, a form that the owner of the site must hand over on demand. The original of the completed form is sent to the provincial office of the Catalonian regional administration or to the State Secretary for Tourism (Secretaria del Estado del Turismo, Calle de Maria de Molina 50, E–28006 Madrid).

Spending one night in a caravan or motor caravan in lay-bys and car parks is allowed but not on the open roads. Camping away from recog-

◀ *A group of stone dancers in front of the amusement park on Montjuïc*

nised sites is frowned upon, not least because of the danger of forest and heath fires breaking out in the dry months of the year.

Through roads usually avoid the old centres of the mountain and coastal resorts. Drivers towing caravans and drivers of motorhomes are advised to avoid these centres because of the narrow streets.

Lists of officially recognised campsites can be obtained from tourist information offices. Otherwise contact:

Information

Associació de Càmpings de Barcelona
Gran Via C.C. 608
E–08007 Barcelona
Tel. 934125955

Campsites

Camping Cala Gogó
E–08820 El Prat de Llobregat
Close to the airport. The sea quality here can be poor.

Camping Masnou
E–08320 El Masnou (11 km (7 mi.) north-east)

Camping Ballena Alegre, Camping Filipinas and Camping El Toro Bravo
E–08840 Villadecans (12 km (7½ mi.) south-west)

Camping Tres Estrellas and Camping La Tortuga Ligera
E–08850 Gavá (13 km (8 mi.) south-west)

Car Rental

Carrer Rita Bonnat 5 (in Les Corts district)
E–08029 Barcelona; tel. 934102038

Avis

Carrer Casanova 209 (in Sarrià district)
E–08021 Barcelona; tel. 932099533

Carrer Aragó 235 (in Eixample district)
E–08007 Barcelona; tel. 934878754

Barcelona Airport (in El Prat de Llobregat)
E–08820 Barcelona; tel. 932983603, 93298360, 932983604

Barcelona Airport (in El Prat de Llobregat)
E–08820 Barcelona; tel. 93298350, 932983503

Budget

Carrer Vilodomat 214 (in Eixample district)
E–08029 Barcelona; tel. 934398403

Europcar

Carrer Consell de Cent 363 (in Eixample district)
E–08009 Barcelona; tel. 934882398

Sants Railway Station (in Sants/Montjuïc district)
E–08014 Barcelona; tel. 934908662

Hertz

Carrer Tusset 8–10 (in Sarrià/Sant Gervasi district)
E–08006 Barcelona; tel. 932173248 and 932178076

Barcelona Airport (in El Prat de Llobregat)
E–08820 El Prat; tel. 932983639 and 932983637

Currency

The unit of currency is the peseta (pta). There are notes in denominations of 1000, 2000, 5000 and 10,000 pesetas and coins for 1, 5, 10, 25, 50, 100, 200 and 500 pesetas.

Euro

On January 1st 1999 the euro became the official currency of Spain, and the Spanish peseta became a denomination of the euro. Spanish peseta notes and coins continue to be legal tender during a transitional period. Euro bank notes and coins are likely to be introduced by January 1st 2002.

Import and export of currency

There are limited restrictions on the import of Spanish or foreign currency (cash or cheques). It is mandatory, to declare large sums of foreign currency (over the equivalent of 1 million ptas).

Exchange

Outside the opening hours of banks (Mon.–Fri. 8.30am–2pm, Sat. 8.30am–12.30 or 1pm) money can be changed in exchange offices, travel agencies, and at larger hotels. Money is changed at the official rate, but a varying rate of commission may be charged.

Traveller's cheques

It is advisable to take money in the form of traveller's cheques. Eurocheques can be made out for up to 25,000 ptas, but are not always accepted.

Cash dispensers

Holders of Eurocheque cards can draw cash from more than 4500 Eurocheque cash dispensers in Spain. Holders of credit cards (Visa, Access, American Express, etc.) can also draw cash from dispensers bearing the appropriate symbol. American Express has more than 150 of its own dispensers which will issue travellers' cheques as well as cash.

Credit cards

Most of the international credit cards are accepted by banks and by many hotels, restaurants and shops.

The loss of a Eurocheque or credit card should be reported at once by telephone to the issuing organisation. The major credit-card companies have emergency branches in Madrid. Any card holder who suffers the loss of a card should phone the following numbers where there is no international facility to cancel. You may reverse the charges.

American Express	915720303 or 915707777
Diner's Club	915474000
Visa	933152512 or (900) 974445

Customs Regulations

EU countries

In theory there is now no limit to the amount of goods that can be taken from one EU country to another provided they have been purchased tax paid in an EU country, are for personal use and not intended for resale. However, customs authorities have issued guide lines to the maximum amounts considered reasonable for persons over 17 years of age. These are: 10 litres of spirits or strong liqueurs; 20 litres fortified wine (port, sherry etc.); 90 litres of table wine (of which not more than 60 litres may be sparkling wine); 110 litres of beer; 800 cigarettes or 400 cigarillos or 200 cigars. There is no limit on perfume or toilet water.

For those coming from a country outside the EU or who have arrived from an EU country without having passed through custom control with all their baggage, the allowances for goods obtained anywhere outside the EU for persons over the age of 17 are: 1 litre spirits or 2 litres of fortified wine and 2 litres table wine; 60 millilitres perfume, 250 millilitres toilet water; 200 cigarettes or 100 cigarillos or 50 cigars or 250 grams tobacco.

Non-EU countries

Diplomatic Representation

Consulate
Avinguda Diagonal 477
Edificio Torre de Barcelona, 13th floor
E–08036 Barcelona; tel. 934199044

United Kingdom

Consulate
Cran Via Carles III 94
E–08028 Barcelona; tel. 934915021

Ireland

Consulate
Reina Elisenda 23
E–08034 Barcelona; tel. 93280222

United States

Consulate
Pg. de Gràcia 77
E–08008 Barcelona; tel. 932150704

Canada

Emergencies

There are emergency telephone boxes along the motorways.
Accident = accidente; breakdown service = auxilio en carretera

Motorways

Emergency number of Policía Municipal (Municipal Police): tel. 092
In conjunction with the Patronat de Turisme the Municipal Police operates a 24-hour emergency service for tourists:
Tourist Attention, Policía Urbana, District Ciutat Vella, Rambla 43, E–08002 Barcelona; tel. 933019060

Municipal Police

Country-wide emergency number of the Policía Nacional (National Police): tel. 091

National Police

Emergency number of Bombers (Fire Brigade): tel. 080

Fire Brigade

Emergency doctor service: tel. 061
Ambulance Service of Creu Roja (Red Cross): tel. 933002020

Doctor

Advice on holiday problems (such as overbooking of hotel, poor service, problems with the tour operator) can be obtained from the Organización de Consumidores y Usuarios; tel. 932180611.

Advice

Events

Cavalcades dels Reis Mags (Three Kings' Day processions; January 4th and 5th)
Festa Major del Barri de Sant Antoni (city district festival; middle of the month)
Start of Monte Carlo Rally for Spanish competitors (end of the month)

January

Events

February	Setmana del Llibre Català (Catalan Book Week; beginning of the month) Carnestoltes (Carnival, in all districts) Festa de Santa Eulàlia (festival of the city's patron saint; February 12th)
March	Setmana Santa (Holy Week, processions) Festa de Sant Medir (Gràcia district festival; beginning of the month) Ralli Internacional de Cotxes d'època (Barcelona–Sitges veteran car rally)
April	Setmana del Llibre (Book Week in the Poble Espanyol) Setmana Internacional de Música Contemporània (Week of Contemporary Music) Diada de Sant Jordi (St George's Day, book and rose festival; April 23rd) Festa Major del Barri de la Sagrada Família (city district festival)
May	Fira del Llibre (Book trade fair; end of the month) Fira de Sant Ponç (traditional honey market in the Old Town; May 11th) Festas de Maig al Districte de Sant Marti (city district festival; beginning of the month) Festivitat de Santa Rita (rose and candle market in the Old Town) District festivals in Sarrià-Sant Gervasi, Sant Andreu, Horta
June	Festa Major de Ciutat Meridiana (Nouse Barris district festival; middle of the month) Revetiles de Sant Joan (Midsummer Night festival in all districts; June 23rd and 24th) District festivals in the Old Town, in Sants-Montjuïc, Sarrià-Sant Gervasi, Horta Festival Internacional del Cinema (international film festival) Festival Grec (cultural festival; early June to early August)
July	Beneddicció de Cotxes per Sant Cristòfol (Festival of St Christopher, blessing of vehicles) Processó Marinera de la Verge del Carme (district festival with procession near the harbour) District festivals in Horta, Nous Barris and the Old Town A Nous Barris Marxa (film and music festival in Nous Barris district; until the end of the month)
August	Festa Major de Sant Roc (St Roch festival in the Old Town; middle of the month) District festivals in Gràcia, Sants-Montjuïc, Vallvidrera and Sant Marti
September	Jornades Internacionals de Cant Coral (international choir festival in Museu Marítim) Festa de Treball (labour festival on Montjuïc; middle of the month) Festivitat de la Mercè (festival of the city's patroness; week of September 24th) Festa Major del Port (harbour festival; middle of the month) District festivals in Guineueta, Sarrià-San Gervasi, Barceloneta, Horta, Sant Marti, Gràcia, Sant Andreu, Sants-Montjuïc and the Old Town Formula I motor racing on the Circuit de Catalunya (end of the month)
October	Festival de Tardor de Barcelona (festival of theatre, music and dance) Festa de la Hispanitat (anniversary of the discovery of America; October 12th) Festivals in all districts Ralli Vehicles Històrics (vintage car rally)
November	Festa de la Música Catalana (festival of Catalan music; end of the month) Festa de Tots Sants (All Saints) Festes de Tardor (autumn festivals in all districts)

152

Festa dels Músics – Santa Cecilia (music festival; around November 22nd)

Festival Internacional de Jazz (international jazz festival; all November)

Dia de la Constitució (day of the constitution; December 6th)   December

Fira de Sant Llúcia (crib in the vicinity of the cathedral; from December 13th)

Festivitat de Sant Esteve (Feast of St Stephen; December 26th)

Excursions

The most important places in the neighbourhood (Costa Dorada, Montseny, Montserrat, Sant Cugat) can be found within the Sights from A to Z section of this guide.

The following recommended destinations are slightly further afield.

The excavation site of the ancient town of **Emporion**, nowadays   **Empúries**
Empúries, lies on the Golf de Roses, about 130 km (80 mi.) north-east of Barcelona. It was founded in the 6th c. BC by Greek settlers, coming under Roman rule in the 3rd c. BC, and was destroyed by the Frankish-Alemannic armies in the 3rd c. AD

The ruins are made up of the Greek lower town and the Roman upper town. The site comprises extensive remains of various buildings, mosaic floors and large water cisterns together with an interesting **museum**. In the Roman upper town, which has still only been partly excavated, there are mosaic floors, a surrounding wall and the limited remains of an amphitheatre.

Figueres is about 15 km (9 mi.) inland from the Golf de Roses. It is the   **Figueres**
birthplace of the Surrealist artist and sculptor Salvador Dali. The principal attraction is the **Museu Salvador Dali** which is accommodated in a former theatre and contains a fascinating collection of works by this exceptional artist.

Girona, the capital of the province of the same name, is about 90 km   **Girona**
(56 mi.) from Barcelona either on the motorway which leads to the Spanish-French border or on the national road which runs parallel along the Costa Dorada. It is situated at the confluence of the Riu Onyar and the Riu Ter and has an impressive historic Old Town, a Gothic cathedral (fine cloisters) and other ecclesiastical buildings. The **Cathedral Museum** houses exhibits of Romanesque and Gothic church architecture; of particular interest is the colourful wall tapestry (11th c.) depicting the history of the Creation. The **Passeig Arqueològic** (Paseo Arqueológico), a marked archeological walk, takes in the most important sites of the Old Town.

The national road 152 leads north to the provincial town of Ripoll in the   **Ripoll**
valley of the above-mentioned Riu Ter about 90 km (56 mi.) from Barcelona and 50 km (31 mi.) south of the state boundary on the Collado de Ares. In the principal square in the heart of the town centre stands the large complex of buildings which belong to the Benedictine monastery of **Santa Maria**. The monastery was completely rebuilt to the same design after being destroyed by fire. The most significant relic is the magnificent main doorway (12th c.) of the Romanesque church. It is notable for the great number of representations of themes of the Old and New Testaments. The cloisters (12th–15th c.) are also noteworthy.

Not far to the east of Ripoll a minor road leads to Sant Joan de la   **Sant Joan de les**
Abadesses with the Romanesque church of Sant Joan (12th c.) that for-   **Abadesses**
merly belonged to a monastery. It houses a carved group depicting the

Descent from the Cross (12th c.) and has interesting cloisters and a museum.

Sant Pere de Rodes

The road from Sant Joan continues to the beautifully situated ruins of the former Benedictine monastery of Sant Pere de Rodes, one of the most important examples of Romanesque architecture in Catalonia.

Ullastret

On the estuarine plain of the Riu Ter east of Girona (see above) is the excavated site of **Poblat Iberic** (Iberian settlement 7th–2nd c. BC), the largest site of its kind in northern Spain. There are extensive remains of the town walls and houses. A museum stands on the acropolis.

Vic

The route to Ripoll (see above) leads to the bishopric of Vic, 60 km (37 mi.) north of Barcelona. On the edge of the Old Town is the great **cathedral** (originally founded in 1040; extensively rebuilt 1803–21 and again following the Civil War). In the choir ambulatory a coloured and richly gilded marble altar (15th c.) with scenes from the life of Jesus and St Peter; in the triple-storey cloisters (Romanesque, Gothic and Renaissance) is the bombastic monument of Jaime Balmes (1810–48), sometime advisor to Pope Pius IX and who is considered the most important Spanish academic of the 19th c. The **Museu Episcopal**, opposite the cathedral, houses an excellent collection of Romanesque ecclesiastical art (sculpture and frescos) together with Gothic and Baroque art treasures.

For more information about the region surrounding Barcelona consult the Baedeker guide "Spain".

Food and Drink

Spaniards have always taken their meals much later than other Europeans, (lunch between 1 and 3pm and dinner as late as 9 or even 10pm) though with the development of the tourist trade it is now usually possible to get lunch or dinner rather earlier than in the past.

The normal Spanish breakfast is a very simple meal, but hotels accustomed to catering for foreign visitors, particularly those in the higher categories, often provide a buffet breakfast offering more substantial fare, which may include a choice of coffee, tea, fruit juice, various kinds of bread, jam, eggs and cold meat.

Spanish meals are usually substantial (hors d'oeuvre, etc., followed by main dish, fruit and cheese). The fixed-price menu (*comida*) of four or more courses is considerably cheaper than eating à la carte. The tourist menu, in three price ranges, consists of three courses: the price usually includes a quarter litre of wine or beer, service and other charges.

Spanish cooking makes much use of olive oil (*aceite de oliva*) and garlic (*ajo*). Egg dishes, rice dishes and fish are particularly tasty and appetising. There are many restaurants specialising in seafood (*marisquerías*).

An alternative to a restaurant meal is offered by the *tascas* (bars), which provide a variety of appetisers (*tapas*) – olives, pickled vegetables, kebabs, ham, seafood, garlic potatoes, pieces of tortilla – often supplied free as an accompaniment to drinks. If you want more you can order a *ración* of the titbits displayed on the counter. In this way, particularly by visiting a number of tascas in the course of the evening, it is possible to make up a substantial and varied meal. An advantage is that the bars are open all the time, while restaurants open only at 9pm and may be full by 10pm. Outside the large tourist centres on the coasts tapas are a very good bargain.

Spanish dishes

Hors d'oeuvres (*entremeses*) include sausage, cold meats, ham (*jamón serrano*), seafood and olives. A Catalonian speciality is blood sausage or black pudding *butifarra* or *butifarron*.

Confectionery to tempt eye and palate

Among Spanish soups (*sopas*) gazpacho is the best known. Served cold, it is made from tomatoes, cucumber, onions, garlic and peppers with vinegar, oil and spices; the diced vegetables are often served separately.

The first main course (*plato fuerte*) is often tortillas (omelettes), in numerous variations both savoury and sweet. The various local dishes combining meat and vegetables are both nourishing and substantial. Among them are *cocido*, a stew of meat, chick peas, bacon, potatoes and other vegetables, the exact composition varying from one part of the country to another. Also excellent when properly made is the well-known *paella*, a rice dish made with chicken, meat, fish, seafood, beans and peas for which Valencia is particularly renowned. It usually has to be ordered for a minimum of two people.

Fish dishes (*pescados*) are a delicacy but are not as abundant as might be expected in a port. *Zarzuela de mariscos* is a stew of different kinds of fish, highly seasoned. Fish are also served as *tapas* (appetisers), particularly eels (*anguilas*) boiled in oil with garlic and pepper. Any kind of fresh fish is excellent simply fried in oil.

Spain has a great variety of desserts (*postres*) – excellent cheeses and a wide range of sweets. *Turrón* (a kind of nougat made with honey and almonds) and marzipan date from Moorish times; and in addition there are pastries (*ensaimadas*), spiced cakes, flan (caramel custard), candied yolk of egg and magnificent fruit.

The preferred Spanish drink is wine. Ordinary table wine (*vino corriente* or *vino de mesa*) is frequently mixed with water or mineral water. For further information on Catalonian wine-production see Wine.

Sangria, a popular refreshing drink, is a mixture of red wine, brandy, mineral water, and orange and lemon juice with cubes of fruit and ice.

Beer (*cerveza*) is becoming increasingly popular in Spain. Beer restau-

Drinks (bebidas)

Bars, popular for snacks

rants (*cervecerías*) serve imported beers as well as the lighter Spanish beers.

Non-alcoholic drinks include a variety of fruit juices as well as mineral water (*con gas* = sparkling; *sin gas* = still). Spanish water is usually heavily chlorinated; a pleasanter drink is spring water, which is not expensive (sold in plastic containers, usually of 5 litres).

Spanish brandy (*brandy*, *coñac*) is a popular drink. To get the full aroma it should be ordered in a warmed glass (*vaso caliente*). This can become quite a ceremony: the waiter warms the glass over a spirit stove, pours in a little brandy and swills it round in the glass over the flame until the alcoholic vapours ignite and fill the glass with a pale blue flame; he then pours in more brandy, which diffuses a rich aroma.

Spanish menu

Miscellaneous		
	cubierto	table setting, cutlery
	cuchara	spoon
	cucharita	teaspoon
	cuchillo	knife
	tenedor	fork
	plato	plate
	vaso	glass
	taza	cup
	servilleta	napkin
	sacacorchos	corkscrew
	bocadillo	sandwich
	butifarra	Catalan sausage
	chorizo	red paprika sausage
	torreznos	rashers of bacon

desayuno	breakfast	Meals
comida	lunch	
cena	dinner	
aceitunas	olives	Hors d'oeuvres
ensalada	salad	(*entremeses*)
ostras	oysters	
anchoas	anchovies	
sardinas	sardines	
jamón	ham	
rábanos	radishes	
mantequilla	butter	
pan	bread	
panecillo	roll	
sopa de legumbres (de yerbas, de verduras)	vegetable soup	Soups (*sopas*)
sopa con guisantes	pea soup	
sopa de lentejas	lentil soup	
sopa con tomates	tomato soup	
sopa de fideos	noodle soup	
sopa de arroz	rice soup	
sopa de pescado	fish soup	
caldo	bouillon	
gazpacho	cold vegetable soup	
huevo	egg	Egg dishes
crudo	raw	(*platos de*
fresco	fresh	*huevos*)
duro	hard-boiled	
pasado por agua	soft-boiled	
tortilla	omelette	
huevos revueltos	scrambled eggs	
huevos frites (huevos al plato)	fried eggs	
huevos con tomate	eggs fried with tomato	
frito	fried	Fish (*pescado*)
asado	roasted	and seafood
cocido	boiled	(*mariscos*)
ahumado	smoked	
a la plancha	roasted on a griddle	
anguila	eel	
arenque	herring	
atún	tunny	
bacalao	cod	
besugo	sea bream	
carpa	carp	
esturión	sturgeon	
gado	haddock	
lenguado	sole	
merluza	hake	
rodaballo	turbot	
salmón	salmon	
sollo	pike	
trucha	trout	
almeja	clam	
bogavante	lobster	
calamar	squid	
camarón	shrimp, prawn	
cangrejo de mar	crab	

Food and Drink

cangrejo de río	crayfish
gamba	prawn
langosta	spiny lobster
ostras	oysters

Meat (*carnes*)		
	asado	roast
	carne ahumada	smoked meat
	carne estofada	stew
	carne salada	salt meat
	chuleta	chop, cutlet
	fiambre	cold meat
	jamón	ham
	serrano	smoked
	salchichón	salami-type sausage
	bistec	steak
	buey	beef
	carnero	mutton
	cerdo	pork
	cochinillo, lechón	sucking pig
	cordero	lamb
	rosbif	roast beef
	ternera	veal
	tocino	bacon
	vaca	beef

Poultry (*aves*)		
	faisán	pheasant
	ganso	goose
	pato	duck
	perdiz	partridge
	pichón	pigeon
	pollo	chicken

Game (*caza*)		
	ciervo	venison (red deer)
	corzo	roe-deer
	jabalí	wild boar
	liebre	hare

Vegetables (*verduras*)		
	alcachofas	artichokes
	apio	celery
	cebollas	onions
	col de Bruselas	Brussels sprouts
	coliflor	cauliflower
	col lombarda	red cabbage
	ensalada	salad
	escarola	endive
	espárragos	asparagus
	espinacas	spinach
	garbanzos	chick peas
	guisantes	peas
	judías	beans
	lechuga	lettuce
	patatas	potatoes
	patatas fritas	chips
	pepinillo	gherkin
	pepino	cucumber
	pepollo	cabbage
	tomates	tomatoes
	zanahorias	carrots

Condiments (*condimentos*)		
	aceite	oil
	mostaza	mustard

pimienta	pepper	
sal	salt	
vinagre	vinegar	
barquillos	wafers	Desserts (*postres*)
bollo	bun	
compota	compote	
dulces	sweets	
flan	caramel cream	
helado	ice	
de chocolate	chocolate ice	
de frambuesa	raspberry ice	
de vainilla	vanilla ice	
con nata	with whipped cream	
membrillo	quince jelly	
pastel	cake	
queso	cheese	
tarta	tart	
torrijas	fritters	
cerezas	cherries	Fruit (*frutas*)
chumbos	prickly pears	
dátiles	dates	
fresas	strawberries	
higos	figs	
limón	lemon	
mandarinas	mandarines	
manzana	apple	
melocotón	peach	
melones	melons	
naranjas	oranges	
nueces	walnuts	
pera	pear	
piña	pineapple	
plátano	banana	
uvas	grapes	
agua mineral	mineral water (*con gas* = carbonated; *sin gas* = still)	Drinks
cerveza	beer (*dorada* = light; *negra* = dark)	
café con leche	white coffee	
café helado	iced coffee	
café solo	black espresso coffee	
horchata	refreshing almond drink	
jugo	juice	
té	tea	
vino	wine (*blanco* = white; *tinto* = red; *rosado* = rosé)	

See entry	Restaurants
See entry	Wine

Getting to Barcelona

Because of the distance between Britain and Spain it is advisable to allow three days for the journey making two overnight stops, although it can be done comfortably by experienced motorists in two days. It should be pointed out that the motorways in France and Spain are subject to tolls.

By car

The mileage can be reduced by using one of the rail services that can take the visitor and their vehicle at least part of the way to Spain; information can be obtained from Rail Europe/French Tourist Office, 179 Piccadilly, London W1V 0BA, or your travel agent.

By air

Barcelona Airport is situated to the south-west of the city in El Prat de Llobregat. The Spanish national airline Iberia and British Airways fly direct from London to Barcelona. Scheduled services between North America and Spain are provided by Iberia, TWA and Canadian Pacific Airlines either direct or via London. There are flight connections, sometimes with a stopover, from all major European airports. Iberia and its affiliate Aviaco operate flights between Barcelona and other Spanish cities.

By train

There are through services from Paris to Barcelona usually travelling overnight; it is possible to leave London late in the morning, change in Paris and travel by the Barcelona Talgo train departing Paris (Austerlitz) at 9pm and arriving in Barcelona about 8.30 the following morning.

For further information see Public Transport.

Hotels

Hotels in Spain are officially classified in various categories according to their function: standard *hoteles* (singular *hotel*) providing accommodation with or without meals usually with their own restaurant; *hoteles apartamentos*, apartment hotels with facilities similar to hotels but with accommodation in flats or bungalows (chalets); *hostales* (singular *hostal*) modest hotels or inns providing accommodation with or without meals; *pensiones* (singular *pensión*) pensions or guest houses with a limited number of rooms, providing full board only.

Hotels, apartment hotels and hostales may also be run as *residencias*, providing only accommodation and usually breakfast.

Hotel Categories

Official	In this book
★★★★★	L (luxury)
★★★★	I
★★★	II
★★	III
★	IV

Luxury hotels in the following list are additionally designated by a red star.

Hostales and pensiones

★★★	PI
★★	PII
★	PIII

Hotel lists

The Spanish Ministry of Economy and Finance, Turespãna, publishes annually a list of hotels and apartments. Also, particularly for the individual autonomous provinces such as Barcelona, lists can be obtained from the local Spanish tourist offices (see Information).

Hotels in Barcelona (selection)

★Clarís, Pau Clarís 150, E–08009 Barcelona, L, 124r; tel. 934876262, fax 934878736

The Clarís, a member of the Association of Small Luxury Hotels of the

World, is conveniently situated near the Old Town and the Ramblas. Designed by well-known architects utilising marble, glass, stone and the finest timber, the hotel is furnished with many period pieces and works of art bought at auctions throughout the world. It has cascades, a Japanese garden and its own Egyptian museum. In addition to several restaurants and a bar, amenities include a roof terrace with pool, a gym, sauna and solarium.

⋆Rey Juan Carlos I, Avda. Diagonal 661–671, E–08028, L, 412r; tel. 934480808, fax 934480607
One of the Leading Hotels of the World group, the Rey Juan Carlos I is located close to the financial district and fashionable shops and affords extensive views of the city. Set in its own garden, it has spacious, comfortable rooms, indoor and outdoor pool, boutiques, tennis courts, health club and more. The Chez Vous restaurant serves mainly French food with a taste of Catalan. The Café Polo is less formal; the Aris Bar is a popular evening rendezvous.

⋆Ritz/Husa Palace, Gran Vía 668, E–08010 Barcelona, L, 161r; tel. 933185200, fax 933180148
In a central position not far from the Barri Gòtic and the Ramblas, this grand hotel with its magnificent façade, lovely interior and spacious rooms, another member of the Leading Hotels of the World group, combines the charm and elegance of yesteryear with modern comforts and exclusive service. In the excellent Restaurant Diana fine continental cuisine is served by candlelight to music from a piano. The piano lounge is the place to meet for afternoon tea, the elegant Parrilla Bar for cocktails.

⋆Arts Barcelona, Carrer de la Marina 19–21, E–08005 Barcelona, L, 455r; tel. 932211000, fax 932211070
Only a short distance from the Nova Icaria Olympic marina and handy for the Old Town and the Picasso Museum, this luxury hotel with terraces, restaurants, bars, swimming pool, gym, sauna, etc. commands a fine view of the city.

⋆Barcelona Hilton, Avda. Diagonal 589–591, E–08014 Barcelona, L, 274r; tel. 934957777, fax 934957700
The Hilton Hotel is situated at the heart of Barcelona's commercial and financial district, 15 mins. from the airport, 10 mins. from the station and 20 mins. from the Old Town and within easy reach of the Exhibition and Congress Centre and main Olympic site. In addition to the tastefully furnished rooms and the first class service expected of a high-amenity hotel, it has a shopping gallery, terrace restaurant, cocktail bar, gym and flexible conference facilities.

Ambassador, Pintor Fortuny 13, E–08001 Barcelona, I, 105r; tel. 934120530, fax 933027977
Only a few steps away from the bustle of the Ramblas and not far from the Barri Gòtic, opera house, old La Boqueria market and port, this elegant hotel is where the Dream Team among others stayed during the 1992 Olympic year. It offers modern comfort and a superb panoramic view from the roof terrace with swimming pool.

Avenida Palace, Gran Vía 605, E–08007 Barcelona, I, 159r; tel. 933019600, fax 933181234
Located near the Ramblas; a classic grand hotel with a magnificent spiral staircase.

Condes de Barcelona, Passeig de Gràcia 75, and Condes de Barcelona Centre, Passeig de Gràcia 73, E–08008 Barcelona, I, 183r; tel. 934882200, fax 934880614

This hotel, conveniently situated near the Ramblas, occupies two buildings facing one another; the façade is protected by a preservation order. Other attractive features include multi-storey inner patios, roof terrace with swimming pool, brasserie, bar and lounges.

Gran Hotel Havana, Gran Vía 647, E–08010 Barcelona, I, 141r; tel. 934121115, fax 934122611

Situated in the business and shopping district between the Barri Gòtic and the church of La Sagrada Família, this hotel with Neo-Classical façade and multi-storey Catalan-style inner patios, is modern and equipped with every comfort.

Barcelona Plaza, Plaça Espanya 6–8, E–08014 Barcelona, I, 347r; tel. 934262600, fax 934260400

Situated in the immediate vicinity of the Exhibition Grounds, this hotel is particularly suitable for people travelling on business. It has more than ten conference and meeting rooms, a restaurant, piano bar, pool and sauna.

Expo Hotel, Carrera Mallorca 1–23, E–08014 Barcelona, I, 435r; tel. 933251212, fax 933251144

Very handily situated right by Sants station and only a short distance from the Exhibition Grounds, this four-star hotel is especially suitable for business people. It has several restaurants, a piano bar, 11 conference rooms, sauna, solarium and hair salon.

Meridien Barcelona, Rambles 111, E–08002 Barcelona, I, 209r; tel. 933186200, fax 933017776

The Meridien, another four-star hotel, stylish, with a friendly atmosphere, lies within easy reach of the city's major sights. Facilities include a restaurant, a piano bar and a small gym.

Rivoli Ramblas, Rambla dels Estudis 128, E–08002 Barcelona, I, 87r; tel. 933026643, fax 933175053

Occupies a restored Art Deco building in the Ramblas; antique and Art Deco furnishings.

Metropol Hesperia, Ample 31, E–08002 Barcelona, II, 68r; tel. 933105100, fax 933191276

In a former palazzo not far from the Passeig de Colom.

Reding, Gravina 5, E–08001 Barcelona, II, 44r; tel. 934121097, fax 932683482

Comfortable, light rooms; cafeteria-restaurant with bar.

Regina, Bergara 2, E–08002 Barcelona, II, 102r; tel. 933013232, fax 933182326

Situated not far from the Ramblas and Plaça Catalunya; large rooms, competitively priced. Restaurant, snack bar and bar.

Information

United Kingdom

Spanish Tourist Office
22–23 Manchester Square, London WIM 2AP
Tel. (0171) 4868077, fax (0171) 4868034

Canada

Tourist Office of Spain
Bloor Street West, 34th floor
Toronto, Ont. M4W 3E2
Tel. (416) 9613131, 9614079

United States

Tourist Office of Spain
666 Fifth Avenue, New York, NY 10133
Tel. (212) 2658822

Tourist Office of Spain
Water Tower Place, Suite 951 East
845 N. Michigan Avenue, Chicago, IL 60611
Tel. (312) 9440216, 9440225/26

Tourist Office of Spain
1221 Brickell Avenue, Miami, Fl 33131
Tel. (305) 3581992

Spanish Tourist Office
8383 Wilshire Blvd., Suite 960
Beverly Hills, Los Angeles, CA 90211
Tel. (213) 6587188, 6587192/93/95

Barcelona tourist offices

Centre d'Inormació Turística de Catalunya, in the Palau Robert Passeig   Catalonia
de Gràcia, 107, E–08008 Barcelona
Tel. 932384000, fax 932384010

Consorci de Promoció Turística de Catalunya (CPTC)
Generalitat de Catalunya
Passeig de Gràcia 112 2n, E–08008 Barcelona
Tel. 932176969, fax 934151434

Turisme de Barcelona   Head Office
(Sants Montjuïc district)   Barcelona
Tarragona 149–157, E–08015 Barcelona
Tel. 934231800, fax 934232649

Gran Vía de les Corts Catalanes 658   Eixample
E–08010 Barcelona
Tel. 933017443, 933172246, fax 934122570

International Terminal   Airport
Aeropuerto de El Prat
E–08820 El Prat de Llobregat
Tel. 934784704, 934780565, fax 934784736

Estació Barcelona-Sants   Sants Station
Plaça Països Catalans, E–08014 Barcelona
Tel. 934914431

Plaça de Catalunya 17 (underground), E–08002 Barcelona; tel. 906301282   Metro junction
(Issuing office for the "Barcelona Card", providing reductions to places Plaça de
of interest and local transport)   Catalunya

Insurance

Calella	San Jaume 231 E–08370 Calella Tel. 937690559, fax 937695982
Sitges	Sinia Morera (Oasis) E–08870 Sitges Tel. 938117630, fax 938944305
Tourist helpline	During the summer months a telephone information and helpline, Teléfono de Información Turistica, operates Mon.–Fri. 9am–8pm. Visitors can obtain tourist information for Barcelona in German, English, French, Spanish and Catalan; tel. 901300600.
Red Jackets	Throughout the summer (June to September) all sorts of tourist information can be obtained from guides (employed by the Patronat de Turisme, easily identified by their red jackets and stickers with the letter "i"), stationed in the Barri Gòtic, on the Ramblas and in the Passeig de Gràcia.
Càtedra Gaudí	For those with specialist interests, access to certain Modernisme buildings not normally open to the public may be obtained by applying to the Càtedra Gaudí located in the Les Corts district, in the Finca Güell (see Sights from A to Z): Avinguda Pedralbes 7 E–08034 Barcelona; tel. 932045250

Insurance

Visitors are strongly advised to ensure that they have adequate holiday insurance, including loss or damage to luggage, loss of currency and jewellery.

Health	Residents of other European Union countries may receive medical care when on holiday in Spain on production of a form issued by their national health service (form E111 for British citizens). Treatment can be obtained free of charge, but up to 40 per cent of the cost of prescribed medicines must be paid, except for pensioners who are exempt. A Spanish doctor must be shown the original form, plus a copy which is retained each time treatment is sought. therefore a number of photocopies should be taken. It is essential for visitors from non-EU countries, and advisable for EU nationals, to take out some form of short-term health insurance providing complete cover and possibly avoiding delays. Nationals of non-EU countries should certainly have insurance cover.
Vehicles	Visitors travelling by car should be ensure that their insurance is comprehensive and covers use of the vehicle in Spain.

See also Travel Documents.

Language

The official language of Spain is Castilian (Castillano) Spanish but most inhabitants of Barcelona prefer to use Catalan (Català), although Castilian is widely understood. Place names on signs in the city are almost invariably in Catalan. In information offices, hotels and restaurants English is generally understood, but even a slight knowledge of Spanish will prove beneficial and the introduction of a word or phrase in Catalan will be greeted with pleasure. Below are some everyday words and expressions in Castilian ("High" Spanish) and in Catalan:

English	Spanish	Catalan
good morning	Buenos días	bon dia
good day (after midday)	buenas tardes	bona tarda
good night	buenas noches	bona nit
goodbye	adiós/hasta la vista	adéu/passi-ho bé
yes/no	sí/no	sí/no
excuse me	perdón	perdó
don't mention it/ not at all	de nada	de res
help yourself	sírvase usted	serveixi vostè
if you please	por favor	si us plau
thank you (very much)	(muchas) gracias	(moltes) gràcies
allow me	con permiso	amb permis
do you speak English?	¿habla usted inglés?	parla vosté anglès?
I don't understand	no entiendo	no ho entenc
have you a room free?	¿hay una habitación libre?	tenen una habitació lliure?
single room	habitación individual	habitació individual
double room	habitación doble	habitació doble
a bath/shower	baño/ducha	bany/dutxa
key	llave	clau
what does it cost?	¿cuánto vale?	quant costa?
the bill/check	cuenta	compte
where is the road ...?	¿dónde está la calle ...?	on és el carrer ...?
street (in a town)	calle	carrer
road (outside a town)	carretera	carretera
motorway/highway	autopista	autopista
to the right	a la derecha	a la dreta
to the left	a la izquierda	a l'esquerra
straight ahead	derecho	dret
above/up	arriba	a dalt
below/down	abajo	a baix
January	enero	gener
February	febrero	febrer
March	marzo	març
April	abril	abril
May	mayo	maig
June	junio	juny
July	julio	juliol
August	agosto	agost
September	setiembre	setembre
October	octubre	octubre
November	noviembre	novembre
December	diciembre	desembre
Monday	lunes	dilluns
Tuesday	martes	dimarts
Wednesday	miércoles	dimecres
Thursday	jueves	dijous
Friday	viernes	divendres
Saturday	sábado	dissabte
Sunday	domingo	diumenge
morning	mañana	matí
midday	mediodía	migdia
evening	tarde	vespre
night	noche	nit

Markets

Municipal market halls

Almost every district has its municipal market hall with an abundant display of fruit, vegetables, dairy products, meat, fish and seafood. Three of the market halls (Mercat de Born, Mercat de Sant Antoni and Mercat de Sant Josep) are of notable architectural interest; they are described in the Sights from A to Z section.

Local markets

In Barcelona there are the following local markets:
Barceloneta (Plaça de la Font), Buen Pastor (Carrer Sant Adrià 154), Canyelles (Carrer Antonio Machado 8), Carmel (Carrer Llobregós – Conca Tremp), Ciutat Meridiana (Carrer Costabona 4), Clot (Plaça Mercat 26), Concepció (Carrer Aragó 317), Encants/Sant Antoni (Carrer Manso-Urgell), Felipe II (Carrer Felip II 118), Fira de Bellcaire (Plaça de les Glòries), Galvany (Carrer Santaló-Madrazo), Guinardó (Passatge Llivia-Oblit), Guineueta (Passeig Valldaura 186), Horta (Carrer Tajo 75), Hostafrancs (Carrer Creu Coberta 93), Les Corts (Travessera de les Corts 229), Lesseps (Carrer Verdi 214), Llibertat (Plaça Llibertat 27), Ninot-Porvenir (Carrer de Mallorca 133), Mare de Déu del Carme (Carrer Cid 10), Mare de Déu la Estrella (Carrer Providència 170), Mare de Déu de la Mercè (Passeig Fabra i Puig 270), Mare de Déu de Montserrat (Via Favència 241), Mare de Déu de Núria (Avinguda Rasos de Peguera 186), Mare de Déu de Port (Carrer Energia 21), Provençals (Carrer Menorca-Treball), Sagrada Família (Carrer de Mallorca 475), Sagrera (Plaça Masadas 6), Sant Andreu (Plaça Mercadal 41), Sant Antoni (Carrer Comte d'Urgell 1), Sant Gervasi (Plaça Frederic Soler 1), Sant Josep/Boqueria (Rambla Sant Joesep 101), Sant Marti (Carrer Puigcerdà 212), Santa Caterina (Avinguda Francesc Cambó 16), Sants (Carrer Sant Medi 7), Sarriá (Passeig Reina Elisenda de Montcada 7), Tres Torres (Carrer Els Vergós 2), Trinitat (Carrer La Fosca 10), Unión (Plaça de la

Mercat de Sant Antoni, the central market on the Rambles

Unió 25), Vall d'Hebron (Passeig Vall d'Hebron 130) and Vallvidrera (Carrer Reis Catòlics).

Motoring

Driving in Spain

In Spain, as in the rest of continental Europe, traffic travels on the right, with overtaking on the left.

At junctions and roundabouts traffic coming from the right has priority. This applies even to side streets in towns; exceptions are signposted.

Priority

For left-hand turns off a main road there is often a marked filter lane to the right which then turns to cross the main road at right angles.

Turning

When overtaking the left-hand indicator must be kept on during the whole process and the right-hand one used when pulling back to the right. The horn must be sounded (or, after dark, the headlights flashed) before overtaking or before a bend. A good lookout should be kept for overtaking lorries. Drivers about to be overtaken should operate their right-hand indicator to show the driver behind that they understand his intention to pass.
    Overtaking is prohibited within 100 m (328 ft) of a blind hill and on roads where visibility is less than 200 m (656 ft).

Overtaking

On well lit roads (other than expressways or motorways) sidelights alone may be used. Beware of unlit vehicles. It is compulsory for motorcyclists to use dipped headlights during the day.
    Motorists in Spain are obliged to carry a spare set of light bulbs.

Lights

In some instances, when changing from green to red, the green light remains on with the amber. Two red lights, one above the other, indicate no entry.

Traffic lights

Parking is permitted in one-way streets only on the side with even numbers on even-numbered days and on the side with odd numbers on odd-numbered days.

Parking

Care is necessary in towns, particularly when the streets are busy in the evening, to avoid pedestrians, who are sometimes reluctant to give way to cars on the roadway. Caution is also required on country roads with relatively little traffic, since country people often pay little heed to the rules of the road.

Pedestrians

Spanish cyclists and motorcyclists often indicate a change of direction by waving an arm up and down, but this does not always make their intention clear: the right arm may be used to give warning of a left turn, or vice versa.

Cyclists

Farm and other animals are often a hazard on country roads. In rural parts of Spain there is often a strip of grazing land alongside the road (even at intersections – a drove road (*cañada*) for travelling flocks of sheep. A loud horn is therefore very desirable.

Animals

Foreign motorists in particular should observe strict driving discipline for the sake of their national reputation as well as for their own safety. The directions of the Policia Municipal in towns and the Guardia Civil de Tráfico (traffic police) should be immediately complied with: if a driver fails to stop when signalled to do so the police may well make use of

Driving discipline

their revolvers, since they are not infrequently on the alert for terrorists. Fines for traffic offences must be paid on the spot, and are high.

Accidents

To call the police dial 091 (throughout Spain).

An accident in Spain can have very serious consequences, including the impounding of the car until any legal proceedings have been completed and the detention of the driver pending bail. It is very desirable, therefore, to have a bail bond (see Travel Documents).

An accident should be reported at once to your insurance company in accordance with the instructions on your green card or other insurance document.

Towing

The towing of broken-down vehicles by private cars is prohibited.

Speed limits

Speed limits are 120 k.p.h (74 m.p.h) on motorways, 100 k.p.h (62 m.p.h) on dual carriageways, 90 k.p.h (55 m.p.h) on other roads and 50 k.p.h (31 m.p.h) in built-up areas. Cars towing trailer caravans are restricted to 80 k.p.h (49 m.p.h) on motorways and 70 k.p.h (43 m.p.h) on other roads.

Motorways

On most motorways (*autopista*), except some stretches around Madrid and Barcelona, tolls are charged – payable at exit points.

Safety belts

The wearing of seat belts both in front and in rear seats is obligatory.

Alcohol

The alcohol blood limit is 0.5 per 1000.

Fuel

Standard grade petrol (*gasolina normal*): 92 octane (not recommended)
Premium grade (*gasolina super*): 97 octane
Lead free (*sin plomo*): 95 octane
Diesel fuel (*gasoleo*) is also available.

A spare can containing up to 10 litres can be taken into Spain without payment of duty.

Road signs

In Catalonia some Catalan spellings are used exclusively on direction signs, but most can be recognised from the Spanish version, e.g. Gerona = Girona, Lérida = Lleida.

Spanish Motoring Organisation

Reial Automòbil Club de Catalunya (RACC)
Josep Tarradellas 14–16
E–08021 Barcelona
Tel. 934109222

Medical service emergency: tel. 932000644
Mechanics: tel. 932000755, 934143040, 934143454

Museums

The museums and cultural institutions listed below are described in detail in the Sights from A to Z section.

Fundació Antoni Tapies
Fundació Joan Miró
Gabinet de Fisica Experimental
Gabinet Numismàtic de Catalunya
Galeria de Catalans il·lustres

Institut Municipal d'Història
Museu Arqueològic de Barcelona
Museu Clarà
Museu d'Art Contemporani
Museu d'Art Modern
Museu d'Art Precolombí
Museu d'Arts Decoratives
Museu de Cera
Museu de Ceràmica
Museu de Geologica
Museu de la Música
Museu de la Ciència
Museu del Calçat
Museu del Futbol Club Barcelona
Museu del Perfum
Museu de Zoologia
Museu d'Història de la Ciutat
Museu d'Història de la Medicina de Catalunya
Museu d'Holografia
Museu Diocesà de Barcelona
Museu Egipci
Museu Etnogràfic Andino-Amazònic dels Caputxins
Museu Etnològic
Museu Frederic Marés
Museu i Centre d'Estudis de l'Esport
Museu Marítim
Museu Picasso
Museu Textil i d'Indumentària

The museums mentioned below are included in the Sights from A to Z section under the entries indicated:

Institut Botànic, see Botanical Garden
Casa-Museu Gaudí, see Parc Güell
Museu d'Art de Catalunya, see Palau Nacional
Museu d'Arts, Indústries i Tradicions Populars, see Poble Espanyol
Museu d'Autómates del Tibidabo, see Tibidabo
Museu de la Catedral, see Cathedral
Museu del Temple Expiatori de la Sagrada Familia, see Sagrada Familia
Museu de les Arts de l'Espectacle, see Palau Güell
Museu del Llibre i de les Arts Gràfiques, see Poble Espanyol
Museu del Monestir de Pedralbes, see Pedralbes
Museu Mentora Alsina, see Gabinet de Fisica Experimental
Museu Militar de Montjuïc, see Montjuïc
Museu Taurí, see Plaças de Toros
Museu Verdaguer, see Casa-Museu Verdaguer

There are also many smaller or highly specialised museums for which either prior appointment is necessary or admission is restricted to specialists.

Col·lecció d'Indumentària de Bomber
(Collection of Fire Brigade Uniforms)
Passeig Nacional 67, E–08003 Barcelona; tel. 933194353

Museu Automóbil
(Vintage Car Club of Barcelona)
Via Augusta 182, E–08021 Barcelona; tel. 932095523

Museu de Criminologia
(Criminology Museum at the Law Faculty of the University)
Avinguda Diagonal 684, E–08034 Barcelona; tel. 932051112

Museu de la Farmàcia Catalana
(Pharmaceutical Museum)
Avinguda Diagonal 643, E–08028 Barcelona; tel. 933307920

Museu del Foment de Obres I Construccions
(Vehicle collection of the Municipal Department of Works)
Carrer Balmes 36, E–08007 Barcelona; tel. 933189000

Museu de Temàtica Espeleològica
(Cave Museum)
Carrer Maurici Serrahima 19, E–08012 Barcelona; tel. 932174802

Museu Geològic del Seminari
(Geological Museum of the Seminari Conciliar)
Carrer de la Diputació 231, E–08007 Barcelona
Tel. 932541600

Museu Institut Amatller d'Art Hispànic
(Museum of Spanish Art)
Passeig de Gràcia 41, E–08007 Barcelona
Tel. 932160175

Museu Oceanogràfic
(Museum of Oceanography)
Moll de Barcelona, E–08003 Barcelona
Tel. 933187749

Museu Odontològic de Catalunya
(Museum of Dentistry)
Carrer Tapineria 10, E–08002 Barcelona
Tel. 933101555

Museu Pompes Fúnebres
(Funeral Museum)
Carrer Sancho de Avila 2, E–08018 Barcelona
Tel. 934841700

Music

Palau de la Música

The most important concert building in the town is the Palau de la Música Catalana (See Sights from A to Z). In this magnificent Modernisme building both classical and modern experimental music is performed and jazz and pop concerts are held; tel. 932681000.

Liceu

The Liceu (see Sights from A to Z), a first-rate opera house with its own orchestral ensemble, was destroyed by fire in 1994, and reconstruction work will continue until late 1999. Until then, performances are being held at other venues; tel. 934123532 or 934121903.

Palau des Esports

The construction of the new Palau des Esports Sant Jordi has meant a change of purpose for the old sports palace (Carrer de Lleida 40). Nowadays it hosts rock and pop concerts with local and international groups.
Programme information tel. 934231541

Other venues

The Caixa de Barcelona (Municipal Savings Bank) and the Caixa de Pensions (Pensions Bank) promote a number of cultural activities including musical events. Further information from branches of these banks.

Guía del Ocio

The weekly guide to events "Guía del Ocio" is obtainable from all news kiosks.

Nightlife

There is an abundance of entertainment in the evenings and at night in Barcelona, from theatrical performances and concerts to pop and rock, and more exotic attractions such as striptease. Full details are contained in the "Guia del Ocio" which is published weekly and which can be obtained from any newspaper kiosk or from hotel reception desks.

Up & Down, Numància 179, Les Corts, tel. 932804608 or 932091700, offers a sophisticated atmosphere for an upmarket clientèle (gourmet food upstairs, dancing in the disco downstairs). Flamenco is among the attractions at El Cordobés, a nightclub in the Old Town (La Rambla 35, tel. 93176653.

Opening Hours

The opening hours for the museums described in the Sights from A to Z section are given in that section. However, these times may be subject to alteration according to seasonal and other factors. In general it can be assumed that the amusement park on Montjuïc is only open at weekends in winter but open throughout the week in summer but closed on Mondays).

As a rule museums are closed on Mondays.

Museums, sights

There are no legally fixed shop opening hours in Spain. In general shops open on Monday to Saturday between 9 or 10am until 1 or 2pm and between 4 or 5pm until 8 or 8.30pm. In summer they often remain open later (especially food shops, tobacconists and some clothes shops).

Shops

The large stores and shopping centres are generally open Monday to Saturday from 10am to 8pm continuously. A few, however, close on Monday morning.

Department stores, shopping centres

Chemists (*farmàcies*; identified by a sign with a green cross on a white background) are generally open Mon.–Fri. 9.30am–2pm and 4.30–8pm, Sat. 9am–12.30pm. Names and addresses of duty chemists open out of normal hours are displayed on notices in all chemists shops, as well as in newspapers.

Chemists

Banks are open Monday to Friday 8.30am–2pm, Saturday 8.30am–12.30pm or 1pm. In tourist areas during the high season they sometimes open in the afternoon.

Banks

Hours when post offices open vary and generally are displayed in the offices. Most open on Monday to Saturday from 9am to 2pm. The central post office in Plaça Antonio López is open Monday to Friday from 9am to 9pm and Saturday 9am to 2pm.

Post offices

Post

Post office

The post office (*correos*) is responsible for mail, mail orders and telegrams, but not for the telephone network (this is operated by Telefónica; see Telephone).

Stamps (*sellos*) are available from post offices and also from tobacconists (*estancos*) which remain open until late in the evening. These are recognisable by a sign which consists of a stylised yellow tobacco leaf and the letter T.

171

International mail should be posted in letter boxes (*buzones*, singular *buzon*) marked "extranjero" (abroad).

Poste restante: letters, parcels and other correspondence can be collected from all post offices. They must be labelled with the recipient's name, preceded by "Lista de Correos", the name of the town or village and the province in brackets. Identification such as a passport is required for collection.

Public Holidays

Official public holidays

January 1st	Any Nou (New Year)
January 6th	Reis Mags (Three Kings)
March 19th	Sant Josep (St Joseph's)
May 1st	Diada del Treball (Labour Day)
June 24th	Sant Joan (St John; king's name day)
June 29th	Sant Pere i Sant Pau (St Peter and St Paul)
July 25th	Sant Jaume (St James the Apostle)
August 15th	Assumpció (Feast of the Assumption)
September 11th	Diada Nacional de Catalunya (Catalonian National Feast Day)
September 24th	La Mercè (celebration of the city's patron saint)
October 12th	Diada de la Hispanitat (Discovery of America)
November 1st	Tots Sants (All Saints')
December 6th	Dia de la Constitució (Day of the Catalonian constitution)
December 8th	Immaculata Concepció (Annunciation)
December 25th	Nadal (Christmas Day)
December 26th	Sant Esteve (St Stephen)

Movable public holidays

Good Friday
Corpus Christi

Public Transport

Metro

Barcelona has an impressive and efficient Metro (underground railway system) which means that all the places of interest are accessible quickly and conveniently. It operates Mon.–Thu. 5am–11pm, Fri., Sat. until 2am, Sun., pub. hols. 6am–midnight.

Fares

There is one standard fare for all single journeys; maps of the underground lines are on display at all stations (see map p. 174). It is worth purchasing a multi-ticket *(targeta multiviatge)* or a one, two or three day ticket *(abonament tempora)* for an extended visit to Barcelona. A higher tariff of charges applies to single journeys at night, at weekends and on public holidays.

Buses

There are many inner-city bus lines. For the tourist the "Bus 100 – Bus Turístic" service (see Sightseeing) is of particular interest. It operates from mid-June to December; a special ticket is valid for one or two days for unlimited travel on Bus 100 and connections to Montjuïc and Tibidabo. Services normally operate 6.30am–10pm.

There are fifteen special services operating late at night and in the early morning. They make frequent stops on the following routes:

N 1: Zona Franca (Free harbour zone) – Plaça de Catalunya

N 2: Collblanc – Plaça de Catalunya – La Verneda

N 3: Avinguda de Xile – Plaça de Catalunya – Montcada i Reixac

N 4: Plaça Catalana – Plaça de Catalunya – Passeig de la Vall d'Hebron

N 5: Plaça de Catalunya – Horta

N 6: Baró de Vivier – Plaça de Catalunya – Poligon Canyelles

N 7: Plaça de Catalunya – Besòs Mar

N 8: Plaça de Catalunya – Avinguda del Tibidabo

N 9: Drassanes – Plaça de Catalunya – Plaça Rellotge

N10: Plaça de Catalunya – Danta Coloma – Plaça de la Vila

N11: Plaça de Catalunya – Pomar

N12: Plaça de Catalunya – Plaça Pere Dot

N13: Plaça de Catalunya – Ciutat Cooperativa

N14: Plaça de Catalunya – Plaça Església

EN: Plaça Espanya – Aeroport.

Transports Metropolitans de Barcelona (TMB)

A map of all public transport routes (Guia del Transporte Público de Barcelona y su Area Metropolitana) is available from tourist offices (see Information) and from the Transports Metropolitans de Barcelona (TMB) at the Plaça de Catalunya, at 43 Ronda de Sant Pau, at Sants main station (see Railway Stations below), and at the Metro station Plaça de la Universitat.

Information

Timetable information regarding TMB is available on tel. 934120000 and tel. 010.

See entry

Taxis

National Railways (RENFE)

RENFE, the nationalised railway company, operates railway services from Sants station (see Railway Stations below) to local destinations (airport and the seaside resorts in the south of Catalonia).

The railway network in Spain is not so developed as in other central European countries but in Catalonia it is relatively accessible; it is constantly being upgraded and modernised. All larger towns can be reached by train. The main lines are from Portbou (border station for France) through the interior via Girona and close to the coast along the Costa Brava to Barcelona and from Puigcerdà (another border station for France) via Ripoll and Vic to Barcelona.
   Owing to the wider guage on Spanish main railway routes (1674 mm) compared with the central European standard (1435 mm) it is necessary to change trains at the French-Spanish border, with the exception of cer-

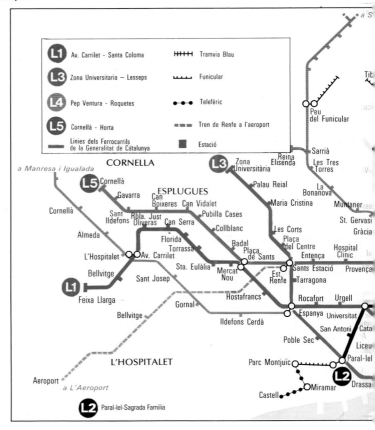

tain international trains with adjustable bogies (see also Getting to Barcelona).

Information

Railway information is available from the RENFE Central Information Bureau (Central de Informació) in Barcelona:

National enquiries tel. 934900202
International enquiries. tel. 934901122

Ferrocarrils de la Generalitat de Catalunya (FGC)

Certain Metro lines are continued beyond the Metro network by the Ferrocarrils de la Generalitat de Catalunya (Catalan Government Railways). There are connections from the Plaça de Catalunya to the foot of Tibidabo, Pedralbes and to Sant Cugat del Vallès, together with Plaça d'Espanya to L'Hospitalet de Llobregat.

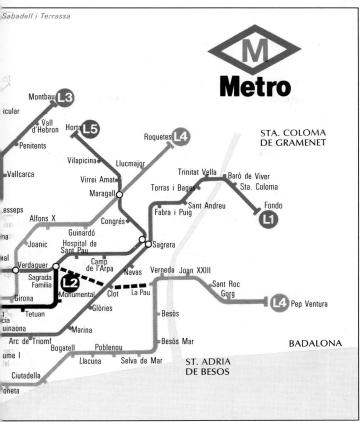

Sabadell i Terrassa

Montbau **L3**
icular
Vall d'Hebron Horta **L5**
Penitents
Roquetes **L4**
STA. COLOMA DE GRAMENET
Vilapicina Llucmajor
Vallcarca
Trinitat Vella Barò de Viver
esseps Alfons X Virrei Amat Sta. Coloma
Torras i Bages
Maragall
Congrés Sant Andreu Fondo
na Joanic Guinardó Fabra i Puig **L1**
Hospital de Sant Pau
Verdaguer Sagrera
Camp de l'Arpa
Sagrada Familia Navas Verneda Joan XXIII
L2 Monumental Clot La Pau Sant Roc Gorg
Girona Glòries **L4** Pep Ventura
Tetuan
uinaona Besòs
Marina
Arc de Triomf Besòs Mar BADALONA
Bogatell Poblenou
ume I
Llacuna Selva de Mar ST. ADRIA DE BESOS
Ciutadella
oneta

Although the trains of the FGC are hardly distinguishable from those of the Metro and they operate from the Metro stations Plaça de Catalunya, Plaça d'Espanya and Diagonal, there is no common fare system so it is necessary to purchase a new ticket when making these connections.

The trains of FGC also serve the region around Barcelona (e.g. via Sant Cugat del Vallès to Sabadell or Terrassa from the Plaça de Catalunya station; the Plaça d'Espanya to Montserrat line passes places of interest to the visitor). The FGC also operates services to destinations inland (Tibidabo, Sarrià district).

FGC information bureau, Pg. Gràcia 26, 7am–9pm: tel. 932051515.   Information

Railway Stations

There are two long-distance railway stations in Barcelona maintained by the nationalised railway company RENFE.

175

The **Estació de França** (French railway), situated on the north-east side of the old town has recently been extended and renovated. With its high-tech equipment, the railway now forms by far the most important transport connection into southern France.

Barcelona central station is the **Estació Sants**, north-west of the Plaça d'Espanya. Long-distance national services to Madrid, Andalucía, Galicia, Valencia, etc. and international trains (including daily services to Paris and Geneva) operate from here. Regional services to the seaside resorts of south Catalonia leave from this station. Trains stopping here also stop at the more centrally located Estacío Passeig de Gràcia, as well as Estació Plaça de Catalunya for connections to Vic, Puigcerdà and la Tour de Carol (for Andorra).

FGC

The local railway network of the FGC operates from the station below the **Plaça d'Espanya**. There are services to Tibidabo via Sant Cugat del Vallès to Sabadell or Terrassa. Services to the south of Catalonia and to Montserrat operate from the Plaça d'Espanya.

Restaurants

As everywhere else in Spanish tourist areas and cities Barcelona has a wide range of restaurants (*restaurantes*) to suit every palate.

Mealtimes

Meals in Spain are taken one to two hours later than in most other countries. Lunch is seldom served before 1pm, and usually after 2pm, whilst in the evening people meet for meals no earlier than 9pm, and preferably after 10pm. Most restaurants remain open until midnight. Hotel restaurants frequented principally by central European and British visitors often go to considerable trouble to meet the eating habits of their guests. There are also many restaurants serving hot food throughout the day.

Many restaurants close Sunday and throughout August.

Restaurants in Barcelona (selection)

★ Neichel, Beltran i Rozpide 16, tel. 932038408
Famous restaurant, one of the Relais & Châteaux chain, located in the centre of Pedralbes, a delightful residential district of Barcelona. Specialises in French and Mediterranean dishes; particularly noted for its huge selection of cheeses and desserts. Regular patrons include well-known politicians, bankers, artists, actors and sports personalities.

★ Florian, Bertrand i Serra 20–22; tel. 932124627
An upmarket meeting place.

★ Reno, Calle Tuset 27; tel. 932009129, 932099180, 932001390
Gourmet restaurant offering French and Catalan cuisine; be sure to book in advance.

★ Vía Veneto, Gandúxer 10–12; tel. 932007024
Regional dishes.

★ Botafumeiro, Gran de Gràcia 81; tel. 932184230
Exclusive restaurant serving excellent fish and seafood dishes.

★ La Cuineta, Paradis 4; tel. 933150111 or 933150812
Situated near the cathedral; antique furniture and Catalan specialities.

★Eldorado Petit, Dolors Monserdá 51; tel. 932045153

Renowned gourmet restaurant in the north-west of the city.

Dive, Port Vell (Maremagnum); tel. 932250150
First-class cuisine and sometimes a show and entertainment in the Steven Spielberg designed submarine interior straight out of a fantasy film.

Planet Hollywood, Marina 19–21 (Nova Icaria); tel. 932211111
First Spanish venture for the extravagant restaurant chain. Rendez-vous of stars from film and show business.

Siete Puertas, Paseo de Isabel II 14; tel. 933193033
Traditional restaurant popular at weekends for family celebrations.

Egipto, Carrer Jerusalem 3; tel. 933173033. Calle Jerusalem 12; tel. 933177480; Rambla 79, tel. 933179545
Catalan specialities.

Agut, Carrer Gignás 16; tel. 933151709
In the harbour district; fish specialities, also good starters and desserts.

Beltxenea, Carrer Mallorca 275; tel. 932153024
Basque dishes in elegant surroundings; alfresco in fine weather.

Los Caracoles, Escudellers 14; tel. 933023185
Country-style restaurant near the Ramblas serving Catalan food and speciality grills.

Gambrinus, Moll de la Fusta; tel. 932219607
Restaurant on the Promenade des Moll de la Fusta where seafood fig-

The Gambrinus fish restaurant

ures large on the menu. Well known for its giant plastic prawn by Javier Mariscal who was also responsible for the 1992 Olympic mascot.

Network, Av. Diagonal 616–618; tel. 932017238
    Hamburgers and light snacks.

El Petit Restaurant Vegetaria, Nápols 330; tel. 932074262
    Vegetarian dishes.

Bodegas (wine cellars, bars)

The friendly, informal atmosphere of the city's *bodegas*, most of which are found concentrated between the Ramblas and the Vía Laietana, make them a favourite with locals and tourists alike. The celebrated *tapas* (small appetisers) are offered with the wine.

Safety

In the main season, especially in Barcelona and the other large centres of tourism, an increase must be expected in thefts. Many a wallet has changed hands in a crowd, especially on the Ramblas, in the Old Town areas and the Metro stations, and the detection rate is small. A favourite trick is to dirty the tourist's clothing from behind, and then to pick his pockets with unbelievable dexterity whilst "attempting to clean the dirt off". For this reason experienced tourists will stand with their backs against the wall in the underground. Another popular method is to place a carnation in the victim's lapel while calling out "Simpatía!" and to rob him while his attention is distracted. It is advisable to avoid "games of chance" which are a common sight on the Ramblas. Cars should not be parked in unsupervised places.

The narrow streets of the Barri Gòtic and Barri Xino are best avoided after dark, especially by unaccompanied persons.

If the police are informed of a theft or that something has been stolen from a vehicle, the victim will be treated with courtesy but will have little chance of any action being taken, for the authorities are simply over-taxed; however, a statement made to the police in the event of a complaint or a theft is necessary to support a claim under insurance. A heavy police presence is obvious in the centres of the drug scene (e.g. Plaça Reial and the Ramblas). They are primarily concerned with preventing violent attacks.

It is advisable always to keep articles of value on the person (identity documents, money, etc.) and to leave large sums of cash and cheques in the hotel safe deposit or in a security box at a camp site. It is also a good idea to have photocopies of passports and other important documents which should be kept separately from the originals. In the event of loss this will greatly facilitate replacement (see Travel Documents).

Loss of
Eurocheques

The loss of Eurocheques or credit cards should be reported at once to the issuing office so that a stop can immediately be put on the account in question.

Emergency
services

See Emergencies

Shopping

Crafts

To get a general idea of Catalonian arts and crafts, visit the Permanent

Crafts Centre of the Generalitat de Catalunya, Passeig de Gràcia 55, and the shops and workshops in the Poble Espanyol on the Montjuãc.

The Bulevard dels Antiquaris in the Old Town, Passeig de Gràcia 55–77, has over 70 shops offering a wide range of goods. **Antiques**

A large selection of books, records, videos and newspapers can be found at Crisol, Consell de Cent 341, and Rambla de Catalunya 81. **Media**

There is a particularly good selection of ceramic work: in Catalonia most of this comes from the town of La Bisbal. The everyday articles of the region are tasteful, practical and inexpensive. In Barcelona colourful decorative tiles painted in designs from the Museu de Ceràmica (see Sights from A to Z) are popular. Beautiful items are sold by Itaca, Ferran 24–26. **Ceramics**

A typical souvenir of Barcelona is the artistic glassware, particularly the charming little ships in bottles made completely from glass. Exquisite gift articles can be bought from Vinçon, Passeig de Gràcia, 96. **Glass**

Spanish silverware is very attractive. In the better shops the visitor can find artificial pearls which cannot be distinguished from the real thing, expertly manufactured by the people of Mallorca. These pearls are certainly not cheap fashion jewellery and are sold not only in Spain but exported all over the world. The most noteworthy brand is "Perlas Majorica". Many jewellery shops are found in the Old Town. **Jewellery**

Good modern leather work (shoes, clothing, accessories) can often be bought directly from the factory. On the Ramblas hawkers' prices should be regarded with due suspicion; there are numerous respectable specialist shops. Plenty of time should be allowed to compare quality and price. Shoes made in Spain can, of course, be obtained in the UK and the advantage in price of buying them in Spain is not very great. **Leather**

Replicas of the exhibits on display can also be obtained from many museums (e.g. Museu d'Art de Catalunya in the Palau Nacional, Museu de Ceràmica, Museu Arqueològic (see Sights from A to Z). **Replicas**

The textile industry in Barcelona is long established and the choice of product is correspondingly wide. **Textiles**

Spain has good and cheap spirits, principally brandy. This is distilled from wine and resembles cognac but is fruitier in taste and has a stronger aroma than its French counterpart. **Spirits**
The best brands are "Duque de Alba", "Cardenal Mendoza", "Lepanto" and "Carlos I"; cheaper brands such as "Veterano Osborne" or "Carlos III" can also be obtained abroad. Aniseed liqueur is popular throughout the country and is drunk after meals – it makes the oily Spanish food more digestible.
For other details about Spanish drinks see Food and Drink and also Wine.

Spanish sweets are popular souvenirs (including all imaginable creations of lollies, candied fruits, nougat and Turkish honey), some of which originated in the time of the domination of Spain by the Moors. The Arabs were (and still are) particularly fond of very sweet titbits, the taste of which is too strong for those from other countries. Ensaimadas, a sweet pastry made of light oatmeal dough and often with a filling, was originally a speciality of Mallorca; small ones are served for breakfast **Confectionery** but larger ones can also be obtained. A visit to one of the larger patisseries is recommended.

Department stores

The large department stores should not be overlooked, such as El Corte Inglés (Pl. Catalunya 14, Av. Diagonal 617–619, Av. Portal de l'Angel 19–20, and Av. Diagonal 471–473).

Shopping streets

The many shopping streets and alleys in the centre also merit attention:

Argentina Center, Avinguda Republica Argentina 238
Aribau, Carrer Aribau 21bis
La Avenida, Rambla de Catalunya 121
Boulevard Rosa, Passeig de Gràcia 55
  Avinguda Diagonal 609–615
  Avinguda Diagonal 474

A delicatessen shop in the Ramblas

Catalunya Center, Rambla de Catalunya 68
Cu-Cu, Carrer Cucurulla 13
Diagonal Center, Avinguda Diagonal 584
Encants Nous, Carrer de València 534
Ferrissa, Carrer Portaferrissa 23
Galeries Maldà, Carrer Portaferrissa 22
Gralla Hall, Carrer Portaferrissa 25
Galerías Halley, Passeig de Gràcia 62
Mercadillo Portaferrissa, Carrer Portaferrissa 17
Piu, Passeig de Gràcia 74
Turó, Carrer Tenor Viñas 12
Urgell Center, Carrer Comte d'Urgell 20
Valencia Center, Carrer València 535–537
Via Wagner, Carrer Bori in Fontestà 17

Maremagnum

The "Maremagnum" complex is a modern shopping and entertainment mall in the port area, where a large number of shops, boutiques, galleries and some restaurants are brought together under one roof (see Sights from A to Z, Port).

Sightseeing

Short break itineraries

1 day

Morning: Barri Gòtic (Cathedral, Museu Marès, Museu Picasso and Museu d'Art Contemporani).
Afternoon: Montjuïc and/or Sagrada Família.

Day 1: as above, opting for Sagrada Família pm.   2 days
Day 2: Montjuïc, with the amusement park, Olympic site, Palau Nacional and Poble Espanyol.

Days 1 & 2: as above.   3 days
Day 3: Eixample, Parc Güell and Tibidabo

Morning: Museu Marítime and Museu de Cera.   Wet weather
Afternoon: Fundaciò Mirò and/or Palau Nacional; alternatively Museu de itinerary
la Ciència.   (1 day)

Transports Turístics

"Barcelona Transports Turístics" operates a circular tour (no guide but information on the tourist bus) that departs from the Plaça de Catalunya and includes the following city sights:

1. Plaça de Catalunya: Oficina de Turisme, Old University and Palau de la Música Catalana.

2. Passeig de Gràcia: Casa Milà, Casa Batlló, Casa Amatller, Casa Lleó Morera, Fundació Antoni Tàpies and Museu de la Música.

3. Sagrada Família: Temple de la Sagrada Família, Avinguda Gaudí and Hospital de la Santa Creu i de Sant Pau.

4. Parc Güell: Museu Gaudí.

5. Parc de la Creuta del Coll.

6. Tibidabo: Museu de la Ciència, Tramvia Blau, Funicular and Parc d'Atraccions.

7. Monestir de Pedralbes with the Thyssen-Bornemisza Collection.

8. Olympic Grounds Avinguda Diagonal: Plaça Pius XII, Palau Reial de Pedralbes (Ceramics Museum), Barcelona Football Club Stadium and Museum.

9. Estació Central de Sants: Parc de l'Espanya Industrial, Parc Joan Miró and Plaça dels Paisos Catalans.

10. Poble Espanyol: Poble Espanyol, Pavellò Mies van der Rohe, Palau Nacional (Museu d'Art de Catalunya; partly closed), Avinguda de la Reina Maria Cristina and Exhibition Grounds.

11. Anell Olimpic: Olympic Stadium, Palau Sant Jordi, Piscina Bernat Picornell (swimming stadium) and Universitat de l'Esport.

12. Montjuïc: cable railway and overhead cablecar, Parc d'Atraccions, Fundació Joan Miró, Castell de Montjuïc, Museu Militar, Teatre Grec and Museu Arqueològico.

13. Monument a Colom and Ramblas: Colombus Monument, Golondrines (harbour tour), Museu Marítim and Museu de Cera.

14. Pla del Palau: Museu Picasso, Museu del Born and Parc de la Ciutadella (Zoo, Museu de Zoologia, Parlament de Catalunya, Museu d'Art Modern, Museu de Geologia).

15. Barri Gòtic: Plaça Sant Jaume, Casa de la Ciutat, Palau de la

Generalitat, Cathedral, Museu d'Història de la Ciutat, Plaça del Rei, Plaça Reial, Teatre del Liceu, Mercat de la Boqueria and Palau de la Vireina.

Visitors can travel around the city by tourist buses ("Bus 100 – Bus Turístic", between mid–June and December), the Tramvia Blau (Blue Tram, sometimes replaced by a bus service), the funicular railway to Tibidabo and the cable and overhead railway to Montjuïc. One or two-day tickets which can be bought on the buses provide unlimited travel on the above means of transport while the ticket is valid. An information brochure is obtainable from the municipal information offices (see Information).

Ruta del Modernisme

The Ruta del Modernisme is an excellent sightseeing tour that takes in the most significant sites of Modernisme, the Catalan variant of Art Nouveau (see Baedeker Special p. 30). The most important points along the way are the Palau Güell, Palau de la Músic Catalana, Casa Batlló, Fundació Antoni Tápies, Casa Milá, the Temple de la Sagrada Família, the Parc Güell with the Museu Gaudí and the Museu d'Art Modern (see Sights from A to Z).

A collective ticket valid for 30 days is available. For more information tel. 934880139 or 932915050.

Taxis

Black and yellow taxis are a comfortable and still reasonably priced means of transport. As there are many taxi ranks they are easy to find. A taxi can be hailed in the street (recognisable by the sign "libre" or "lliure" or a green light on its roof) or ordered by telephone 933577755, 933581111, 933001100, 944902222, 933300300 or 932250000. They are equipped with meters.

It is advisable to make a note of the exact address of the hotel and the nearest road junction to it as the name of the hotel alone is insufficient for even the most knowledgable taxi drivers.

Supplements are payable for waiting time, journeys between the centre and the airport, port and railway stations, and for carrying pets or larger pieces of luggage.

Telephone

Telephone numbers in Spain are nine digits. When phoning from abroad dial the international code for Spain 0034 plus the telephone number. To phone the United States or Canada from Spain dial 001 followed by the area code and number.

International calls can be made from telephone kiosks with the sign "internacional" using 100, 200 or 500 peseta coins. Telephone cards (*tarjetas telefónicas*) with values of 1000 or 2000 pesetas for use in card phones, can be purchased in tobacco shops (*estancas*) and savings banks. Cheap rate calls are available between 10pm and 8am on week-days, after 2pm Sat., and all day Sun.

Telephone calls from the hotel are charged at a considerably higher rate than normal.

Theatre

Although there is no national theatre in Barcelona at present there are about twenty-five venues of various sizes. Theatres are situated in the districts of the Ramblas, Avinguda Parallel, Montjuïc, La Ribera and Passeig de Gràcia.

Developments taking place in the city include the Catalonian National Theatre on the Plaça de les Glòries. It will house two theatres and a concert hall with the auditorium (two concert halls with library and Museum of Musical Instruments) next door.

The weekly listings guide "Guía del Ocio" (in Spanish, but the essentials are recognisable) is obtainable from all news kiosks.

Guía del Ocio

See Music

Opera

Time

During the winter months (October to March) mainland Spain and the Balearic Islands observe Central European Time, e.g. one hour ahead of Greenwich Mean Time: six hours ahead of Eastern Standard Time in the United States. During the summer months (end of March to end of October) the clock is advanced by one hour. The dates are published in the press.

Tipping

Although in hotels and restaurants the service charge is included in the bill, it is usual to tip the waiter (*camarero*), chambermaid (*camamera* or *muchacha*) and other personnel (mozos), especially when some particular service has been provided. Waiters in restaurants expect 5 to 10 per cent of the bill, but in bars less than 5 per cent of the change received is sufficient.

Taxi drivers, usherettes at theatres, cinemas and bullfights expect a tip, so that it is advisable always to have some small change.

Travel Documents

Visitors from the UK, the United States, Canada, Australia and New Zealand must have a valid passport. No visa is required by nationals of Australia and New Zealand for a stay of up to one month, and the UK, United States and Canada for a stay of up to three months provided in each case they are not taking up any paid employment. An extension of stay can be granted by the Spanish police authorities. Children under 16 years of age require their own passport or else must be entered in one of their parent's passports.

Personal documents

A national driving licence is accepted in Spain if it is of the pink EU type, otherwise it must be accompanied by an official translation stamped by a Spanish consulate; it is probably easier and cheaper to carry an international driving permit (available from motoring organisations). The car registration document must be carried as well as an international insurance certificate (green card), and a bail bond (issued by an insurance company with green card) should be taken out, since in the event of an accident the car may be impounded pending payment of bail. The oval nationality plate is required. It is advisable to take out comprehensive insurance when hiring a vehicle as third party insurance in Spain only covers personal injury; a deposit is not usually necessary.

Car documents

An official vetinerary certificate including immunisation against rabies (translated into Spanish) is required for the importation of dogs and cats into Spain. Immunisation should not have taken place less than 30 days or more than one year prior to travelling.

Pets

In view of the quarantine regulations concerning the import of live animals into the UK, British visitors are advised to leave their pets at home.

Advice

It is advisable to prepare copies of passports, driving licence, E111, etc., before departure and to keep these separately from the originals. If papers are lost a photocopy makes it easier to obtain a replacement.

See Motoring

When to Go

The best time for visiting Barcelona is late spring and early summer or autumn. In high summer, during the school holidays, the place becomes so crowded that obtaining accommodation without pre-booking can be a problem. Summer heat is moderated by winds off the sea, but the air can become oppressive in parts of the inner city of Barcelona owing to emissions from cars and industry.

Wine

Although Spain has a greater acreage of vineyards than, for example, Italy or France it is of less importance internationally for wine production. However, export production is increasing and following Spain's entry into the European Community the classification system corresponds to European standards.

Catalonia

On the lower south-eastern slopes of the Pyrenees there are surprisingly very few vineyards and their produce has little importance outside the region. The largest wine-producing area of Catalonia is to the south of Barcelona, centred around Tarragona. Here the emphasis is on the production of red wine, the greater part of which is sold as blended wine. However, Catalonia is renowned for the production of sparkling wine.

Drinks

See Food and Drink

Youth Hostels

Young people will find reasonably priced accommodation in Youth Hostels (*albergues juvenils*). Members of national youth hostel organisations affiliated with the International Youth Hostels Association can normally use the hostels from July to September. For an individual a stay in a hostel is limited to three nights; in the high season previous booking is advisable.

Information

The International Youth Hostel Handbook (volume 1 for Europe and the countries bordering the Mediterranean) is issued every year and is available in Britain from: YHA Mail Order Department, YHA Adventure Shops, 14 Southampton Street, London WC2E 7HY.

Youth Hostel in
Barcelona centre

Hostal de Joves de la Ciutadella
(at the Parc de la Ciutadella)
Passeig Pujades 29
E–08018 Barcelona
Tel. 933003104

Other youth
hostels

Alberg de Montserrat
(in Gràcia district)

Carrer Mare Déu Coll 41–51
E–08023 Barcelona
Tel. 93210515

Alberg Kabul
(in the Old Town)
Plaça Reial 17
E–08002 Barcelona
Tel. 933185190

Alberg Pere Tarrés
(in Les Corts district)
Carrer Numància 149
E–08029 Barcelona
Tel. 934102309

Alberg Studio
(in Sarrià-Sant Gervasi)
Duquessa d'Orleans 58
E–08034 Barcelona
Tel. 932050961

Index

Principal Sights of Tourist Interest

Imprint
84 colour photographs, 14 drawings, 10 ground plans, 5 special plans, 1 general map, 1 special map, 1 inner city plan, 1 transport plan, 1 large city map

German text: Peter M. Nahm, Ostfildern, Vera Beck, Aichtal

General direction: Rainer Eisenschmid, Baedeker, Stuttgart

Cartography: Harms, Ingenieurbüro für Kartographie, Erlenbach; Falk Verlag, Hamburg (large city map)

English translation: David Cocking, Crispin Warren, Julie Waller, Wendy Bell, Margaret Court, Rosemary Quinton

Source of illustrations: Archiv für Kunst und Geschichte (3); Baedeker-Archiv (3); Lade: Dass (1); Museu d'Història de la Ciutat de Barcelona (1); Nahm/Pfaffinger (67); Schapowalow (2); Scherenbacher (2); Skupy (2); Zefa: Santos (2)

Front cover: Tony Stone Images. Back cover: AA Photo Library (P. Wilson)

3rd English edition 1999

Published by AA Publishing (a trading name of Automobile Association Developments Limited, whose registered office is Norfolk House, Priestley Road, Basingstoke, Hampshire RG24 9NY. Registered number 1878835).

Distributed in the United States and Canada by:
Fodor's Travel Publications, Inc.
201 East 50th Street
New York, NY 10022

A CIP catalogue record of this book is available from the British Library

Licensed user:
Mairs Geographischer Verlag GmbH & Co.
Ostfildern-Kemnat bei Stuttgart

Printed in Italy by G. Canale & C. S.p.A, Turin

ISBN 0 7495 2200 3

Notes

Notes